The Disobedience of the
Daughter of the Sun

Other books by Martín Prechtel

Secrets of the Talking Jaguar
Long Life, Honey in the Heart
Stealing Benefacio's Roses
The Unlikely Peace at Cuchumaquic

The Disobedience of the Daughter of the Sun

A Mayan Tale of Ecstasy, Time,
and Finding One's True Form

Martín Prechtel

North Atlantic Books
Berkeley, California

Published by
North Atlantic Books
Huichin, unceded Ohlone land
aka Berkeley, California

Cover and interior art by Martín Prechtel
Cover and book design by Suzanne Albertson
First published in 2001 by Yellow Moon Press
Printed in the United States of America

The Disobedience of the Daughter of the Sun: A Mayan Tale of Ecstasy, Time, and Finding One's True Form is sponsored and published by North Atlantic Books, an educational nonprofit based in the unceded Ohlone land Huichin (*aka* Berkeley, CA) that collaborates with partners to develop cross-cultural perspectives; nurture holistic views of art, science, the humanities, and healing; and seed personal and global transformation by publishing work on the relationship of body, spirit, and nature.

North Atlantic Books's publications are distributed to the US trade and internationally by Penguin Random House Publisher Services. For further information, visit our website at www.northatlanticbooks.com.

Library of Congress Cataloging-in-Publication Data

Prechtel, Martín.
    The disobedience of the daughter of the sun : a Mayan tale of ecstasy, time, and finding one's true form / by Martín Prechtel.
        p. cm.
    "Sponsored by the Society for the Study of Native Arts and Sciences"—T.p. verso. Summary: "The retelling of a seminal Mayan tale, with layered commentaries from the author leading the reader to an understanding of the sacred story's deeper meanings and its relevance for contemporary society"—Provided by the publisher.
    ISBN 1-55643-600-9 (pbk.)
    ISBN-13: 978-1-55643-600-0
1. Mayas—Folklore. I. Society for the Study of Native Arts and Sciences. II. Title.
    F1435.3.F6P74 2005
    398.2'089'9742—dc22   2005011407

9 10 11 SCI 25 24 23

CONTENTS

Introduction
  The Urgency of Water   I

The Old Village Friend
  Some Suggestions on How to Read this Book   7

The Story   II

Five Layers of Understandings of the Story   73

  First Layer: Iridescent Tail Feathers
    The Outer Wrappings of the Story   75

  Second Layer: In a Net of Stars
    The Indigenous Understanding   89

  Third Layer
    Ecstasy and Time   117

  Fourth Layer
    Never-Before-Seen Bird   135

  Fifth Layer: The Ecstatic Voice
    A Revolution of the Watery Soul   139

Author's Note   143
Glossary of Mayan Words   145
Acknowledgments   153
About the Author   161
About the Illustrations   163

For the Watery Soul

Introduction

The Urgency of Water

There are stories, other stories and still different stories; there are myths, legends, fairy tales, folktales and many others. Who could say what kind of story this, *The Disobedience of the Daughter of the Sun,* might be?

Kept alive for centuries in the Guatemalan highlands by the Tzutujil Maya from the village of Santiago Atitlan, this story and others like it are not the regular stories. They are not the easy stories; they are not folktales. Perhaps they are mythological, but on the other hand, they're not that either. They are the special stories.

What can be said about them is that they are alive, and being alive they are not just told at any time, but only in the dark. Though everyone by a certain age knows a version of these living stories, only certain people, those accepted storytellers, can tell them and will admit to their knowledge of them, for it is in the telling only that these stories live, and being ancient, big and hungry, they must be brought alive well.

Another thing that we could say is that these stories are from the other world, the invisible world, the world of life-giving spirit out of which these types of stories come clicking and clanking as bare bony frames of themselves until the storyteller, the "word maker," *Bney Tzij*, refleshes each story, "re-membering" it back to life using the everyday life of the village world to dress the bones.

Like an exquisite reoccurring dream whose origins are lost and foggy upon our awaking, whose ending is the beginning of the next dream, these old Mayan stories, though told over and again, always have their beginnings in a previous tale while their endings are in themselves the cliffhanger beginnings of another story to be related at a different time.

After years of listening, a young person learns to recognize her life in the stories and is guided through life by the piloting examples they contain. After becoming an adult, one realizes that there really is only a single, huge, hidden story trunk of which all the others are only magnificent branches, leaves or fruit.

The tales like *The Daughter of the Sun* are the cherished home-style versions of otherwise very sacred mythologies, the kind that are told in the home, outside the ritual cloistering of initiations and such. Though not taboo, they are shown the same great respect as living heroes. And like all villagers, who visit only after the day's work is done and the sun is down, the story visits only at night and mostly in the dry season between November and April, known as the nighttime of the year. The usual time to hear these tales outside the

2

ritual space occurs after the extended family is lying about the central hut having recovered their breath and composure from the iron-smelting, steam-cleaning heat of the weekly *touj,* or steam bath, all of which occurs after dusk before midnight.

Like everywhere in the world, it is the old-time people who are gently courted and coaxed into volunteering one of these many traditional tales after the bath and cold feast that follows.

When first living in the village of Santiago Atitlan, as I did for so many years, I loved the ritual bathing in the fierce heat of the *touj,* and afterwards eating lime-soaked fish and corn cakes, then leaning back with the glowing and happy clan of my ex-wife's family to listen to one of the older uncles bring life to one of these stories.

I was greatly disappointed, though, because I never got to hear the ends of any of the sixty or so ancient mythic tales on account of the relaxing effects of the sweat house, late-hour food and the lulling effects of the old storyteller, which would consistently put the whole household, including myself, into a sound sleep right where we were lounging. Sometimes even the storyteller, his head thrown back, would still be snoring loudly at dawn by the ashed-over embers of the previous evening's cooking fire while the rest of the village roused itself for work.

In a determined mission to hear the final episodes of those stories, I avoided the relaxing sweathouse for awhile, slept late into the morning of the night it was planned, and drank several pots of good Guatemalan coffee just before the storytelling took off. It was a hopeless effort, for in every instance, by the time the Sun Father had crowned his rosy head out of the night's horizon in the east, the tale had still not finished. Because stories like these are not told while "the Father watches," meaning the sun is up, the storyteller would have to stop talking, courteously excuse himself and in a state of unfair exhaustion accrued in his old bones by my greed and unwitting ignorance, drag himself home to the day's challenge.

It turned out that people were supposed to fall asleep listening to these ancient stories, because the stories themselves come from the great collective dream of the "Big Story," and upon hearing whatever fragment of the "Big Story" was being told, our own individual "branch" of dreams on that great tree of the united dream of the "Big Story" would glide right into the comforting flow of the big dream oozing through our sleep. Our souls rode the horse of these old stories right into our own dreams.

In every story of this kind there were convenient stopping places by which time most normal people would have drifted off and the poor storyteller could go home. There I was in my greedy, American right-to-know attitude, trying to hear the end of something which has no end, doesn't want to end and whose beginnings are the ends....

Becoming less addicted to scarcity, I learned quickly enough after that; and years later when I became an initiator, I too was able to remember the same stories back to life right in with the rest of those beautiful, highly opinionated, well appointed, tobacco-skinned, gesticulating word masters.

To me these Mayan stories are like water. To the Tzutujil there is only one water which rushes, puddles or is captured in a multitude of diverse forms like plant leaves, hot springs, rivers, lakes, ponds, ice, tears and streams, and like the amniotic flood at our births, all this water is trying to get back home to the original mother of life, the Great Grandmother Ocean, the great dream pool.

Like water then, there are many, many forms of stories, more than anyone of us could ever know, but like the rivers and tears, each story contains the exact same storywater as the great original "Big Story."

Like life itself, the secret oneness of the "Big Story" is in the overwhelming details of its diversity, where every little person, beast, wind and misery is a necessary part of a greater churning dream. Every story is a dewdrop in the ocean of the "Big Story."

If, as the Mayan language implies, our lives are really trees, then like water, it is the devoted urgency of the real stories to move toward their origination; their willingness to remain trapped en route home as stories in the dryness of our wood that brings us that precious spiritual lifeblood, causing the nutrients of cultural memory to reach the diverse branches of all peoples.

Coveted and stored by the gnarled and convoluted roots of our indigenous beginnings, these roots dig beyond our sight and times into the original churning dream ocean to capture this storywater there as well, causing it to surge into the trunks of our days and the branches of our dreams.

These kinds of stories are the memory that causes us to remember ourselves back into human form. They are not just the memory of what was, but also the memory of what we are surrounded by today.

The extreme and reckless pruning of this tree of life by a culture where television, advertising, media, academia and politics pander to the least common denominator; where people are not loved for their depth, but for their thinness, has left our dreams damaged. The sap of subtlety, this lifeblood of metaphor and myth is rushing spilt and trashed into a wasteland of white noise and canned laughter, with no branches to feed or flowers to force into the seeded fruit of cultural renewal.

But it need not be this way, I think, because despite all of this, a great revolution of the heart and mysterious subtlety is upon us, too subtle perhaps for the machine-minded to detect, comprehend or react in fear. There is a great longing in people all over for stories once again.

As a toast to those people and that possibility, I offer this Tzutujil Mayan story, with my fierce belief that the wounded trunk still lives, willing to flower once again with real stories. Though the enormous branches of our valuable indigenous memories in the form of stories have been cut away and lost, the sap of dreams yet flows. Where the saws and shears let off, our dreams and stories must begin.

The Old Village Friend

Some Suggestions on How to Read this Book

Though small, like Mayan villagers themselves, *The Disobedience of the Daughter of the Sun* is my attempt to give every reader an old village friend, like those aged conversationalists from the 1970s village of Santiago Atitlan, who though they have all gone on, kept alive in me during that magical time what I, in my hopeful grandiosity, would now keep alive in others.

This book, besides being a teacher to those who would visit this old storyteller to learn the deeper things, is always glad to see you,

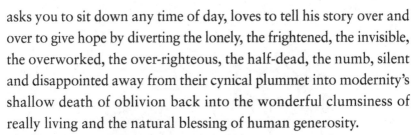

asks you to sit down any time of day, loves to tell his story over and over to give hope by diverting the lonely, the frightened, the invisible, the overworked, the over-righteous, the half-dead, the numb, silent and disappointed away from their cynical plummet into modernity's shallow death of oblivion back into the wonderful clumsiness of really living and the natural blessing of human generosity.

Though people all over the world since forever have had the common experience of seeing their lives unfold as a series of dramatic initiatory passages and changes, it is only a recent development by the advent of modernity's objectivism that psychology has claimed exclusive territorial rights to what this unfolding means and what to do about it.

But, as the village friend of this storytelling book points out, learning to live well, not just to survive, is a constant preoccupation common to all people, and for this the people in the village say that the "story" is the real expert. Every lesson learned from such an expert stays in the story and is not extrapolated out of the story, but remains alive in our lives, because our lives lived out together is the story.

In keeping with this way of living and learning, the reader is encouraged not only to read the entire book but, after reading the story part out loud to someone or quietly to themselves, to begin slowly reading, sentence by sentence, the chapters of "layers" that come after, thinking over each idea in sequence, until he or she arrives at a place that doesn't lend itself to an easy comprehension. At this point, instead of skipping ahead or reading further, the reader must go back and reread the entire story of *The Disobedience of the Daughter of the Sun* again, continuing to read forward, again into the same chapter until reaching the place of previous obstruction. By this time, often in an almost miraculous way, the necessary understanding will have entered and digested the knowledge sufficiently to allow the reader to proceed forward like a leaf floating down a stream toward the ocean, until snagged again on some important obstacle for which the process is repeated until the book has been absorbed.

This form of learning approximates as well as possible the luxurious condition of the cultivation of knowledge found among the old-time Tzutujil Mayans, and probably all intact indigenous people, who after hearing such a story apply it quietly to their own lives until the proceedence of their lives come to a place where understanding doesn't come clear in reference to the tale. They then petition in a courteous moment the good will of sacred storytellers to speak the story back to life once again. After listening carefully, the sequence of increased depth of comprehension is renewed.

If *The Disobedience of the Daughter of the Sun* is embraced in this way, read until the entire book has been inhaled, then my gift to the reader will have been received, and together both the reader and myself will have done some little bit of what we can in these strange times to move away from throw-away culture and keep alive and feed the organic human treasure that has always kept us alive through the ages: the magnificent life-giving gift of a real story.

The Story

Most old folks say this all happened long ago, like twenty thousand years past, while others, just as old, will argue that it was more like two thousand years ago. There were white-haired, street corner mystics who would shake their polished canes, certain that none of it had happened at all, but was on the verge of coming true at any moment.

The great old storyteller Ma Coche, who said he received his power of story from having been horribly bitten by a *Qan Tí,* a fer-de-lance snake, for which he shook uncontrollably for forty years until he died, told me this story was happening as we speak.

Fine old Ma Paqach, so skinny he couldn't cast a shadow, had a grandmother who'd been as thick as he was thin. She claimed to have been there when it all came about and that none of it was anything like anybody ever said.

Ma Xcop Cochenan said he had actually met the Daughter of the Sun personally and was present for the whole story, but then he also said he had a set of matched dueling pistols that shot lightning, which were given to him personally by the Rain Gods themselves, with which he could shoot the great stone bells that used to hang on the summits of all the volcanoes surrounding Atitlan. They'd go ping and blang, ringing out to call the Gods, who'd make it rain. He said he got their attention with the lightning guns.

For my part, I have no idea when any of what follows took place, but when it did, this is what they say happened.

Right here on the lakeshore, where we sit today, just a few centimeters beneath this surface of volcanic dust, a village once stood. It spread out big beyond us to the volcanoes in a maze of little roads and boulder-littered paths which were lined with thick stands of ancient family compounds of magnificent stone huts, deeply thatched and palace-like.

Just five fingers beneath us, under the dust where our village stands today, once stood this Town of Gods owned by the family of the Sun Father. Though called the Village of the Sun, the Sun was married to Grandmother Moon who everyone knew actually ran the place.

After eight hundred years of marriage, more or less, the Moon gave birth to a baby girl who grew up in the village of her father, the Sun. Then she grew some more to become the tallest teenage girl anyone had ever seen, and that was pretty tall, because her parents, being sky Gods, were very long to begin with and she'd already outgrown them all.

But what the world remembered was her beauty. She was not just beautiful like some people think of beautiful, for her beauty was not just for herself. It was a kind of beauty that didn't kill or isolate. She made everything and everyone that saw her or that she saw, touched or walked over want to live a little longer just from the hope of seeing her again. The world flowered and grew wherever she passed. When she brushed them by, wild orchids and lilies mutated into forms and colors never seen before. Even rocks would sparkle, split and crumble into smaller chunks, then grow their ecstatic fragments back into cliffs, defying time and geology, and all because they felt her sueded feet step upon them.

The Daughter of the Sun had no malice in her bones and no awareness of the impatience of envy; she was to be forever the prize of the Village of the Gods.

As she grew deeper and taller, unique, powerful and ripe, she stood so much apart from all the rest that when her mother, Grandmother Moon, sent her on an errand to the lake to fetch water in a heavy, red clay jar balanced on her head or to petition this or that from another family's compound, all the villagers on her route, old and young alike, jumped up to the basaltic boundary walls to get a glimpse of the much admired and highly envied shimmering girl as she floated past.

And that's the way girls have done ever since when they come of age. Because of what the Daughter of the Sun did when she came into her tall teenage years, village girls today dress up in special clothing that they weave themselves, then shining and shimmering, walk the village pathways on their way to fulfill many serious errands for their elders in hopes the village looks upon them with as much regard as it did when Tall Girl roamed the same pathways of the same village dust. Perhaps one of the boys from an admiring family would be attracted to her and she as much to him. Beyond all this, what each girl hoped might happen was what Tall Girl desired as well: to be seen, admired and accepted on her own for what she had become: a young woman, no longer a little child.

But unlike all the girls who came ever after, the Tall Girl was the daughter of a God and of a Goddess; and to the Moon, who was the boss, and to the Sun, who roamed the sky and was the biggest God of all, there was no boy good enough for their girl. According to the Moon, her mother, she must marry only someone of equal status and of equal height. But because her father and her mother were the greatest and most powerful of all, there was no one for her, and none was ever searched for. Not only was she too tall for everyone, but no other woman, not even the Moon, her mother, could match Tall Girl's splendor or her ability to weave, grind, cook, grow things, embroider or generally create, and as such, there was no male on the solid earth to match her female greatness with a male magnificence of equal capacity, subtlety and depth.

Therefore despite all her excellence and the admiration of everything on earth, she was relegated to live out her life in an eternal moment of frustrated possibility and desire that could never find a home.

So, unlike the girls ever after, she threw away her teenage years. In an effort to forget her yearning, she turned the longing of her loyal heart into a flowering whirlwind of work, which she dedicated to feeding, clothing, preparing the home and attending to her parents' every need in their supernatural duties. The Tall Girl's only joy was the pride she felt working without a thought to her own happiness to keep the Sun and the Moon in the sky.

That this most beautiful and powerful girl would never be allowed a specific mate made all the things in the world and all the villagers in the Village of the Sun feel equally in possession of her attention. Just the thought of her beauty in the hearts of those who could never have her kept the whole world moving toward the unspoken possibility of possessing her, though no suitors came and no one was ever rewarded with her hand.

Though he was a God, and the king of the Gods on top of that, the Sun was, like all village men, a working man who, instead of cutting trees, hoeing fields or fishing from canoes in the lake, was a committed servant to the creation in which they all lived. Without his committed hauling of the heated Day throughout the sky, all time would cease and life would be impossible, the entire creation would have collapsed into the mouth of those eternal alligators of oblivion always gnawing at the corners of the universe.

Like a village man, the Tall Girl's father rose early each morning, loaded his back with the sun and climbed up the sky, onto the Sun's road, an ancient trail paved with leaves of blue liquid jade.

To the Sun, the sky is a mountain where one slope is called morning and the opposite the afternoon. In the midday when he reached the summit of the peak, he sat down beneath the chocolate bean tree that grows there in the umbilicus of the sky and waited for the Moon to bring him his lunch.

For this reason, the people all say the Sun doesn't move for a while at its highest point at noon, but holds there for half an hour until once again loading up the heavy brightness of Day, the Sun walks stiffly and concertedly down the opposite slope, into the jaws of night, past the volcanic peaks of the western horizon.

When he arrived back in their royal compound, the Moon, his wife, and the Tall Girl, his daughter, would be ready and waiting with gourd dippers and great, ornate earthen tubs of fresh water. Due to the great heat of what he carried and the toil and danger of the day, the Sun came home as a grimy, lumbering, overheated, hungry kind of grumpy giant. The family knew how a working man such as he needed immediate cooling before he was allowed to talk, after which he could enter, having avoided saying and doing things he'd later regret.

They poured gourdful upon gourdful of cool water over his heated head, which sizzled and popped raising a boiling bank of thick clouds and steam that swelled and curled into the purple night.

After they'd bathed and dried off the poor old beast, they walked him into the House of the Moon where they fed him, and only then did the Sun speak, transformed again into a beautiful God whom the girl knew for her father.

The Tall Girl's mornings were spent splitting wood and starting the universe fire in the hearth of the House of the Moon from the embers of the night's stars. She'd boil the corn at night with lime and ashes, wash it in the sieve at dawn, grind the soft kernels into dough and clap the paste into perfect moonlike rounds that she'd toast on the hot morning griddle until she had a basket full of several hundred corn *wai*. Though some days greens, and some days fish, sometimes birds and on other days tomatoes with smoked wild meat, every day she cooked a different fare from ancient recipes, the aroma rising with the steam from ornate earthen pots made just for the Sun.

Finely arranged in a staggered spiral pattern, the corn cakes and the food filled up a wide basket. Bundled into a cloth covered with the magical live embroidery of the Tall Daughter, these very foods were the meals that the Moon, her mother, every morning carried on her head as she swayed up the great mountain of the sky to meet her husband at the noon summit, spreading the lunch with him alone under the chocolate bean tree.

When he had eaten and had carefully laid the long gourd emptied of *pinol* upside down into her basket, the Sun held her, said goodbye, and loaded with the bright heat of Day, began his steep afternoon descent into the jaws of evening.

The Moon, meanwhile, returned the way she'd come, retracing her steps back down the morning-side slope to the village where she would always find her inspired daughter hard at her daily weaving, which had to be completed every day before the Sun came home.

Other than her daughter, there was no woman more beautiful than the Moon. And besides Old Man Fire, there was no one on earth as old as she. But the Moon was the first of those kind of women for whom age is more a sculptor, carving the young girl's original smoothness into a more complex and deeper beauty.

Still more so for the Moon, as her skin never wrinkled or grew old, and her eyes shone as clear as her teeth were white. Though they didn't show to look at, unless she spoke, that girl's mother had tusks instead of teeth like those of a jaguar, an alligator or a peccary.

Her wrap-around skirt, rippling like iridescent serpent scales, reached clear to the ankles of her feet, beneath which the village paths were swept behind her as she walked by her even longer, thick, white hair, which was so dense that it kept from view the rough tip of a reptilian tail dragging there between her voluptuous feet.

She was wild, noble, scary and full of secrets. Unlike her daughter, whose beauty the whole world beamed to behold and be held, the Moon was a forceful queen, both changeable and fierce, and nothing dared defy her will. More feared than loved, she was definitely obeyed.

But no matter how strange they are to anyone else, at home our parents are just our parents, and for the Daughter of the Sun it was no different. Despite the fact that her father was the Sun and her mother was the Moon and both of them were feared, revered and very different beings outside the home, to the girl they were her beloved parents for whom she was the brightest thing in their lives.

It was for them that she worked so hard, trying to forget her longing for what could never be. She never questioned that decision made without her opinion by her haughty parents.

What she was left with that actually gave her joy was to weave long strips of ornate tribal cloth on her backstrap loom. That's what rang out from the Sun's palatial thatch hut. Anyone passing by could hear the sound of her banging batten, the ringing of the shed opening and the shuttled thread thrown, thundering through as she wove what no one else could manage.

By the time she'd grown into a seventeen-year-old beauty, the Daughter of the Sun had come to be such an expert weaver that from her fingers onto the cloth, the figures she made appear actually came alive. Unlike the fine embroidered clothing of today's village where water bugs, jaguars, eagles, butterflies, rainbows and lightnings are crowded in static rows, wing to shoulder all over the cloth woven by our mothers and sisters, the Tall Girl's creations were moving. Her butterflies flew inside the cloth, her jaguars ate fish and rolled on their backs and snored. The trees flowered and fruited in a myriad of well-imagined colors and on and on. Some even say that she wove the world into life; that the bewildering foment of flowers, fish, breezes, birds, mammals, rivers, plants, clouds, stars and the entire world around us was the imagination and deftness of the weaving heart and hand of the Daughter of the Sun and Moon.

No matter what some might say, what was true is that in her tight strips of weaving, animals moved and lived and plants watched them. The weaving was alive. Anyone walking down the village paths with a blouse or shirt made from one of her magical weavings, made in her efforts to forget her longing for a love, would be wearing the living world churning on their backs.

Every day after splitting the wood, making the fire, washing the corn, grinding the food, the corn and her hopes, hauling the water from the lake in a clay jar on her head, washing out the grimy hardship of their day's struggle in the sky out of the clothing of the Sun and Moon, cooking the corncakes, she would spend the remainder of the day weaving life into her cloth until just before the Sun came home, when the cooking began again. Work was her whole life, working to forget her pain and working to insure the love and admiration of her parents which she pretended to substitute for the impossible love of a sweetheart.

Nobody ever says how it happened or when it happened or where it happened, but it happened that the Daughter of the Sun had some-how fallen in love.

Because she was so popular, so beautiful, royal and tall, the Daughter of the Sun, like her father, was always visible and under the greatest public scrutiny, on top of which she worked all the time, making it all the stranger that neither the world nor the village noticed for the longest time, how every day, in the late morning, just after the Grandmother Moon had padded up the hill to see her husband in the sky, a young and shiny, undersized man with beau-tiful little ears came boldly to visit the Daughter of the Sun.

Though he only came up to her knees, her sweetheart was as courteous as she was magnificent. He shone with a green brilliance, which in the right light sparkled iridescent, in bad light slightly golden. A master of delicious words, his origins remained as hidden as his presence in the girl's heart, for being so small, he could hide, and being so beautiful, the girl didn't waste the short, secret time she had with him discussing trivial rubbish like one's background.

How they originally came to love each other is unknown, but ever since then they would meet everyday in the midmorning. Blending into the shadows along the rocky path beneath the Sun's luxurious compound of palatial thatched huts, the Short Fellow waited out the mornings hiding from the old Grandmother Moon, who with her single purpose, tusks, long hair and tail would brush out the stone threshold and sail out of sight to scale those miles up the great hill to her husband's side for the midday meal.

Jumping from shadow to shadow, from under one overhang to the next, and after making certain the Tall Girl was alone, Shortboy began to whistle a birdlike phrase, a song that the Beautiful Girl had herself taught him to use. If the coast was not clear, she would toss some cloudy cooking water onto the ground as a sign for him to stay hidden. Otherwise the young lady would gracefully emerge to sit opposite him on the sun-warmed black stones of the threshold.

Thus out in the open, not hidden or with shame, she'd watch the little man with beautiful little ears scale the jumbled boulders to the top, where he posted himself, dangling his two bare calves over the edge, rocking them back and forth. But only after she was seated opposite on the earth were they at each other's eye level, so tall she was and short a man was he.

They never touched each other at all. They didn't seduce each other, they didn't want to, because they were already sure of the love each bore the other.

What they did do for hours was to lose each other fast and far inside the other's eyes in a deep road of longing so well paved with respect that when they did speak it was not the speech of smallness, jokes or artful conversation, but a language of courting. They established for us a way of speaking where the force of their mutual loves' desire made a corridor between the two of such magic and poetry that the force field of art and delirious possibility spoke the world into life. This language of courting is the same majestic tongue used by prayer-makers, shamans and other keepers of the majestic and the Holy when they make their rituals.

The girl courted him and the boy courted her, each taking turns, magnificently failing in the most earnest attempts to express the ever-widening depth of feeling each had for the other.

Though one was short and the other tall, they were the same in that neither was like any other. The girl, her eyes the wide, whiteless eyes of wild deer, so natural and deep that the boy almost died drowning in them, drove him to whisper in a clear never-before-heard voice, "When I saw you, I thought a million sky-colored cotingas and more red-breasted bluebirds were rising from a canyon, but I think I was mistaken for it was the fragrant vapors of your life-giving breath fanning the rippling waves of the lake that is your heart . . ."

And in her turn, gazing into his funny round eyes stuck in his shiny little head, the Beautiful Girl spoke, "When I heard your whistling, I sprouted into a leaf who longs to be rolled tight and smoked into your chest, where like a cloud I'd play like a young otter, splashing in the liquid jade of your heart, jumping up to lick your shine like a puppy licks the face of a messy child . . ." And on they'd go, on and on, speaking and gazing, gazing and speaking each other into life. But then because they mustn't be discovered, and in recognition of the Moon's habitual return at the same moment every afternoon, with tears in both their eyes, the girl would reluctantly drift back to her work and the boy to nobody knows where. She didn't even know his name, but she didn't care because she knew him.

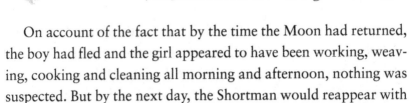

On account of the fact that by the time the Moon had returned, the boy had fled and the girl appeared to have been working, weaving, cooking and cleaning all morning and afternoon, nothing was suspected. But by the next day, the Shortman would reappear with new poems and she with a more enchanted gaze which everyday intensified the depth and excellence of their mutual desire beyond their imaginings.

But the girl knew it could never be, for the boy was far too small, too short, too strange, unknown, unpapered, unemployed, too beautiful, too different. And as thrilled and inspired as she was at his daily comings, just as equally sad and despondent she grew in his absence knowing the truth of the impossibility, hoping to see him all the sooner each day.

But as everybody knows, the Sun and Moon don't really run together and coincide, such that every year, at some point Grandmother Moon comes home early, having quarreled violently with the Sun.

And on such a day the fierce old lady Moon showed up, unexpectedly, midmorning, returning from a vicious battle in the sky with that brute of a workaholic husband, the Sun, only to see as she rounded the bend, in the threshold of her compound, the unthinkably disobedient daughter of her moronic husband gazing slackjawed into the eyes of a little low-life, too short to call a man.

Having muttered all the way home in such an awful disposition, searching for any inconsistencies against which to toss the rancor of her angry humiliation and necessity for revenge, the Moon unleashed a withering barrage of rage and vicious abuse toward the couple which whipped the air with crashing sparks of static electricity.

She bared her tusks, flailed her tail and rushed like an alligator to crush the Little Man, who disappeared like the thoughts of wind to nobody knows where.

The Tall Girl shook and sobbed in shock and grief to see the destruction of the delicious reverie of her courting, which further infuriated the Moon, whose jealousy of her daughter's happy face was even greater than her attachment to the hatred she bore the girl's father.

Bellowing like two-hundred-thousand territorial jaguars, hissing like one venomous snake two million light-years long, she sizzled and shattered the ancient air of then, right here in that village, three inches beneath where we live today.

"What? Who do you think you are spreading your whore-legs for that rat-sized-avocado-licking-shit-of-a-dog-penis-cowardly-zero-of-nothing?" But the girl yelled back too weakly, "But mother, he's beautiful, he ..."

"Beautiful? Beautiful? You're a whore, a slut, a pig's heart, a puta, a nothing!" Over and over in a fit the Moon clawed up fistfuls of earth and began throwing dust throughout the world, spinning all the while, twirling about, gnashing, popping her jaws and snapping at the air. Her tail flailing about, she took to pounding the poor girl with her fists, rubbing dirt into her hair, screaming all the while, trying to crush her daughter's spirit while her daughter continued to weep as she remembered her shiny, little sweetheart who couldn't help her now.

"You're nothing, absolutely nothing, noooooooothing, AHHH-HHHHHHHHHHHHHHH ...," the old woman roared.

"Mother, I love him," the girl spoke back.

"Love him? Him? Him? How can you love something that can only lick your knees. Well?!!"

The girl went silent and the old woman yanked her wrists, dragging her around like half-dead prey. "Answer me, you idiot, you've ruined everything!"

Reeling to dodge another slap to her swelling face, the dust-encrusted, tear-streaked child blurted back to the Moon, "But,

Mother, we did nothing, we didn't even touch, we just spoke, nothing more."

"And speech is nothing to you?"

Like a crazed peccary, the old woman clenched her jaws, popping the joints, grating her ivories with a subsonic grinding rasp so harsh and penetrating that from the otherwise placid lake, waves as tall as day were slapped up by the tortured air and driven so hard upon the growing reeds and shallows that a million ducks, frogs and water bugs were drowned and scattered on the shore; and whispering past her tusks she continued more in a well-enunciated hiss than a tone of speech.

"Can't you remember that you are the child of the *Ajaua*, the Deities, whose very speech makes all things happen? You're tall, you're big, you're father's tall and the most important being of his kind, and I, your mother, am the Moon. We are all meant only for big things, not the stupid little things you hang out with. Our lives are not our own to do with as we please, in our bigness we serve more than our whims. Our very actions, breaths and thoughts make or break the world. Our speech makes winds rise or trees to wither and burn. How can you, idiot girl, expect me to care anything at all for you when you've thrown away and ground to putrid dust all that we grand beings are, just for your desires? All you do is think of yourself."

Chilled by the winds of her mother's hatred and by the shock of being hated for the first time, the defeated girl held herself and shivered, the vapor of her broken heart frozen in a cloud of dreams whose rain soothed the Moon's scorched earth.

"Get inside, get dinner ready for your father and don't speak to me. We'll see what he has to say about all this, maybe his relatives can think of a better way to punish you."

The Sun of course had heard it all, for even in the Village of the Gods, everyone knew the color of your pee before you pissed, had an opinion about it and twisted the story before one had the chance to pee it.

So by the time the girl's father reached the holy threshold of his house, the threshold of dusk, on the other side of which his angry wife and stunned and beaten daughter waited; he crossed it, overly informed, overheated from his job, overworked, tired, very hungry, dreading what he might find.

But when he did, his daughter came to greet him and like every day poured gourdfuls of clear water drawn from clay tubs over the Sun's exhausted, glowing head, causing cautious steam to curl into a torpid mist that crept over the evening land. Then she walked him to the hut where sat his wife, the Moon, like a cat just waiting for the time. Though the tension ran high, the world inside was quiet as the mother and her child washed the feet of the white-haired Sun in water warmed by the fragrant fire, where rose the smell of what Gods like him loved to eat, well cooked by the Daughter of Day and the Eye of Night. He prayed that a meal was forthcoming, but as soon as his great gnarled toes were dry, the old woman started in.

"Do you know what your daughter was ..."

"Is there anything to eat?" the Sun interrupted.

"Of course, yes, there is food, of course, but can we discuss your daughter ..."

"Of course, yes, we can, but is there anything to eat?" the starving and stalling God of Dawn insisted, and as he did, his daughter served him a bowl of stewed water birds and thick corn cakes from which the steaming aroma alone could have staunched the tired man's raging hunger.

The Sun, who dragged his meal out for as long as he could manage, intended to doze off immediately, sleeping like a dreaming man, as the earth does sleep in the sunless night digested in the bowels of the crocodile of oblivion, and then renewed and reassembled by dawn, rises early as the Heart of Day, never once missing a day of work, climbing up over the mountains and down the sky as he'd promised long ago.

But tonight he wouldn't sleep, for the Sun, with his copper eyelids only half lifted, was forced to listen as the Moon recounted the entire story of their daughter's felonious misdeeds with one short boy from nowhere. After a couple of hours of eyebrow lifting at the appropriate parts of the story and uttered groans of disapproval, the Sun's vague disappointment was gradually heated into indignation by the exaggerated case created through the calculating eloquence of the Moon.

"A tiny boy, you say?" he interrogated the girl. "Who are the parents of this fellow anyway? I've never heard of such a being in the entire creation!" Kneeling and peering to the earth, the girl did not reply. The Sun continued to goad his daughter further, "Who is he and where does he come from?"

"I don't actually know, Father."

"What? What? You don't know? He can't be one of us, he's too short, he must be from very far away. What did he tell you?"

"I never asked him and he never told me."

Slapping his belly with one hand, his forehead with the other, the impatient Sun exclaimed, "*Hee yach*, you don't know? You never asked him? Well, what's his name then, at least that?" Like the Moon, he believed that the girl was more deeply involved than she admitted and was deliberately withholding the identity of her lover to protect him.

"I don't know that either. Why does that matter, *Tata*? Father, all I know is that I love him."

"*Cho jic naban kawatet.* 'You just keep carving heads for us to talk to, your fabrications don't form words or truth.' You're trying to hide his identity. *Majun xtincut achí chiq.* 'I'll no longer search your mouth for real words, knowing that you lie and exaggerate.' I'll have to straighten you out on this."

"Honestly, Father, I swear by your heat and my life as your child that I have no idea where he comes from, who his parents might be or if he even knows himself. All I know is that he's a speaker of delicious words and that he is my sweetheart. I don't care about anything else."

The Sun, in a more constant smoldering rage, to the jealous Moon's delight began to lose his stirrups, as she had early on. But instead of screaming and punching, he issued commands and punishments, preferring the calculated, slow burn torture of enforced situations to the uncontrolled wildfires of the heart.

"I'll teach you to care for more than just yourself. You must forget this shameless invader, this nameless nothing, this worthless untier of knots, this small cheeping, joint-loosening, height-leveling, unwashed, unemployed termite. Let him go. You're made for tall things, grand beings, kings, people whose names are known, who can be seen, things not hidden. If I see you speaking to this lowlife ever again, I'll have him killed. Therefore, if you love him as you say, to save him, you must forget him, push him away, otherwise he'll be destroyed by your attentions; we will be watching you from the sky, my brothers and I."

To enforce his will the Sun and Moon now did what had never occurred to anyone before, which was to block up the doorway. From then on, before the Grandmother Moon left on her daily mission to feed her husband the Sun high upon the middle mountain of the sky, the angry Moon would plaster up the doorway with mud and boulders to make certain that no one else would enter and the girl could never leave. In that village there were no doors, only doorways and thresholds, and to close or lock a door could not be done. Thus, they decided to keep her cloistered, hold her captive like a slave, dam her up like a pond, like a lake, like a river, remove her face from the world and more especially keep her from her short and nameless sweetheart.

Then every afternoon, returning from the hills, to get inside the hut, the Moon, muttering and snarling like a badger, was forced to tear apart the very fortress she had expertly created earlier that morning. Boulders would thud, the Moon would pant, grunt, swear, eroding away the wall with her powerful arms. Then once inside bristling and hissing like a tarantula, she threw her daily frustration of having to build and break the wall as well upon the daughter, sinking her verbal claws into the softness of the child, whose heart, though thoroughly mauled, felt it only as the continuation of another long day of grief and sobbing.

Her tears and ragged, unkempt appearance never softened the heart of the hard glaring Sun nor the cold jealousy of the Moon. They now demanded of this weeping child the completion of a daily task she'd been doing for years out of honor and without urging. They commanded that she weave the world into life on her backstrap loom, in larger spans than ever with an intricacy never seen before. By inspecting the distance she'd woven in a day both parents could be sure she'd been hard at work and not mumbling through the walls of the daily dungeon of their home to some no-good short person.

Every morning when, as always, the Moon left, before walling up the entrance with boulders and lime, she'd watch her daughter hitch the unwoven end of her *kiem,* or backstrap loom, to the Y-shaped guy ropes which were bound fast to the middle of some stout, smoke-encrusted overhead beams that held up the tall thatched roof.

Harnessing herself into the rig, the Beautiful Girl, dusty and unwashed, kneeled and leaned back against the loom, raising the tension, tuning it up and brushing it like a harp, and then began the rhythms and forceful picking, shoving, pulling and beating of which she of all women was the expert for all times. Only then did her mother finish damming her in, then waddle off, her rigid thoughts comforted by the rhythmic sound of her captive daughter's industry.

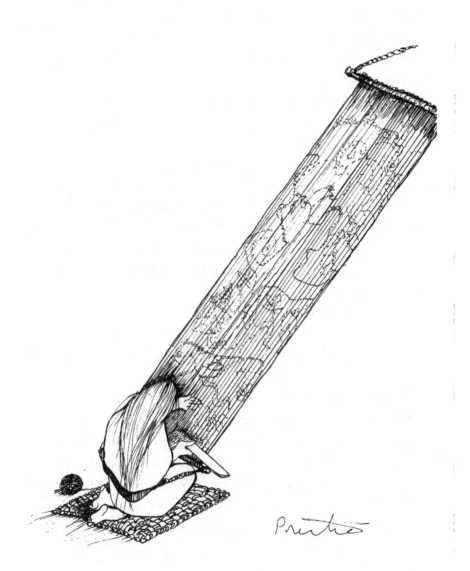

The girl wept as she wove, dropping tears on the tense cloth which rang like the tiny drumming of the first rain of spring; when she thumped the batten toward her to bring the weft tight into the warp, the whole house rang like thunder that was heard throughout the Village of the Sun.

Everything that heard the rumbling of her weaving and the weeping of her heart wept along inside, so much they all did love her, even the relatives of the Sun. Every stone and tree, all the animals and deities pitied her sentence and hated her parents' brashness, but nowhere was there any being who felt justified or powerful enough to denounce the madness of their king and queen.

Remembering the poems of her lost little sweetheart, and for all the confusing time alone, she wove and wept each day away until once again her mother, growling and boring into the wall, returned to berate her and inspect the progress of her loom. In every case the cloth was better than before. A great deal was accomplished for in that cloth the girl had directly woven her losses, the loss of the love of her parents and the Shortman, the loss of freedom, the loss of admiration, the loss of feeling useful to the management of the sky.

She wove all of this into the cloth, but because the Moon was how she was and the father too busy with the Sun's work, no one noticed that the wide cloth had invisibility woven directly into it.

Though the designs she put there jumped, flew, breathed and ran as always, their brightness and magnificence were only on the outside. No one had imagined that what she wove was a cloth, a cape, that could make the wearer disappear, where the living designs in the cloth blended with the everyday things and functions of the world, thereby hiding the wearer within.

It was the rain of her eyes that had tear-soaked the weaving, that had caused it to happen.

When she finished one, she began another. And though she wept through the night and continued despondently, the parents thought that because she applied herself so obsessively to her art, their reform plan was beginning to work.

On and on it went, the Sun returned, ate and slept, and the Moon complained, still jealous that her daughter had so much feeling for her lost love.

The girl had been a major part of the function of the family of the sky, and now all that was broken, confused and sad. Famous for her diligence, she had never done anything for her own renown but for the family of the Sun and the Moon. The lives of these two arrogant celestial lights had been made that much smoother and richer by the Tall Girl's ingenuity, hard work and brilliance, supplying them as she had always done with shining cloth, on-time food, cooking fires, mopping the sweat off her hard-working parents. Now she was hated for her love. Because of her love for one small, beautiful, unknown man, she'd lost the love of her parents. Little by little they were becoming just the sun in the sky and the moon in the night.

The little Shiny Man seemed to have disappeared, which deeply sorrowed the Tall Girl but relieved her as well, knowing full well he'd be blown to bits by the Lightning Brothers of the Sun if she spoke to him. The Sun wouldn't kill him if she didn't talk to him.

Though the Sun's family was a hard, powerful lot, consisting of twelve brothers who were weather Gods, most of them were sympathetic to the girl. Unwilling to interfere in what each perceived was every family's right to do things as they saw fit, they were also afraid of their oldest brother who was lord over all they knew. All except one, who had no love for the Sun.

Known as Q iq and banished by his own disgust of the green flowering Earth, he was a loner who inhabited an unknown quarter farther north where he ruled as the wind and the lord of Dry Times. Having no children, no wife, no sweetheart, no companion, nothing loved him or understood him, nor did anything want to.

When he blew, Q iq dried the world. If the sky chanced to rain while the northern wind blew, it was called the piss of the North Wind because that rain killed and didn't make life live and drove everything into old age. Bitter about the Sun for his famous and successful life, he was particularly jealous of the Sun's beautiful, tall daughter.

Of great vigor, strength and age, he was a law unto himself, and nobody much tangled with him. He blew about as he wished. Penetrating the Sun's hut as a small northern wind, Q iq discovered one day the secret of Tall Girl's cloths of invisibility, and because he was never consulted, recognized or sought after, Q iq kept the girl's secret to himself.

Weeks went by, the girl wept and wove, the Moon left and trotted home only to discover the girl more despondent than before. One morning after the Moon had blocked up the threshold and left for the sky, a small bird could have been seen flying in and out of the luxurious eaves of overhanging thatch, which roofed the palatial hut where the Daughter of the Sun and Moon was cloistered.

No bigger than the first digit of your finger, the world might have mistaken the bird for a bumble bee except that it flew in wide, growing circles, zooming in a kind of fish-like motion on account of a long snake-like iridescent tail, feathers that flashed and fluttered like two tiny banners.

He came every day, bumping into the upper course of lashed cornstalk walls of the enclosure, sounding like a mob of junebugs who are notorious for their inability to take tight turns, causing them to hit whatever presents itself. Good thing they are so armored.

The little bird kept bumping and thumping every day while the Moon was absent, raising a subtle but constant commotion that eventually accumulated into an irritating presence that the girl found she could not ignore, and she finally rose to peer through the slits in the upper cornstalk walls to discover what kind of unknown beast could be making this quiet type of ruckus.

From the walls of carefully fitted carved stone at the height of the shoulders to the wooden roof supports above, standing vertically for eight feet or so was a rack of wooden poles along each wall, over which were lashed with maguey fibers the thick bottom stalks of the substantial, giant corn of the ancients, three layers deep.

Though light enough to permit the thick smoke of a cooking fire to slowly ooze into the sky, these upper walls were so tight that you could barely see through the slits. The Tall Girl pushed her face up against the stalks, searching and staring until the little whirling creature bumped and hovered immediately in view of where her beautiful eye peeked out.

She'd never seen such a strange, shining miniature bird and truly nobody else had either. His beak was as long as his body and made of thin obsidian needles. Besides his shimmering red mask, the rest of him was iridescent green from his neck to the tip of his fluttering tail.

Beguiled by its beauty, she forgot a little the hopeless life she'd been living. Disobeying reason and her parents, Tall Girl began to bore a little peephole in the stalks, enlarging it with her weaving pick until it was large enough to let the little bird squeeze through and fly into the hut. Her loneliness and great desire for a friend made her long to possess the tiny, shiny animal, turning her initial fascination into a desire that had the divine power to pull things toward her. For the first time in months, she actually smiled when the funny, wriggling head of the beautiful bird struggled past the pith and stalks into the dark room where he took off, flying around as crazily as he had outside.

He buzzed right past her face, dive-bombed and did spinning loops over her head, intimidating her brooding heart into an increasing curiosity until, like a cat with some wounded, buzzy thing, standing close, she began to run and laugh, then jump and trip in a hundred vain strategies to grab him who seemed so close. She was determined now to catch that wild, feathered bug and hold its sparkling in her hand.

Just as the little beast was to allow himself to be caught by the Tall Beauty, the great thudding and muttering of the Moon returning from the hills came ringing through the ground, and out squeezed the bird through the hole it had entered and was gone.

The girl, scared but no longer quite as sad, plugged the little tunnel with the gum she'd been chewing, sticking a little corn leaf over the protruding bits to camouflage the conduit and its plug from the immaculate scrutiny of her divine parents.

Though upon entering, the old woman noticed that her Tall Girl had not woven as much, nor as meticulously as usual and that the cloth was not as tear soaked, along with the fact that she seemed less despondent, the Moon thought it all to be a hopeful sign that the girl was in the process of forgetting her boy and all her self-made troubles.

The following day, after the Moon was gone, her daughter unplugged the hole in the wall and the bird returned at once to give chase again, flying into her face, then hovering, then zinging off in and out of range, maintaining his long-tailed roller-coaster buzz and groan. She could never quite capture him and again he would leave when the Moon was heard to come. After several days she stopped chasing him and returned to her loom over which the quetzalito hummingbird would hover. The Tall Girl, much amazed by his presence, began to weave images of him into her cloth.

Passersby could hear her when she began to mutter to the bird, who attentively listened perched on the end of her shed stick. Every day she spoke at length to the little, never-before-seen humming-bird, explaining all her troubles and the details of her existence, something she'd never done before for fear of disgracing her people to outside forces.

The Moon was suspicious when the image of the quetzalito, a never-before-seen-bird, appeared in the girl's traditional weaving of all creation. How could an animal that didn't exist in this world, the imagination of the Gods, show up in her weaving?

Though the Sun only wanted food and sleep and couldn't be convinced of his daughter's further malfeasance, the Moon, going on rumors she'd heard in the streets of the one-sided conversations of her locked up daughter, tried to surprise her daughter by sneaking home early from the mountains and actually heard her daughter inside the hut mumbling animatedly about her life, but by the time the boulders had been tumbled out of the doorway and the jealous old Moon had carved her way into the hut, the adroit sparkling bird had already vanished through the little cornstalk hole. The Moon scrambled, prowled and inspected the room in a vicious focus and finding nothing, turned to the girl, "To whom were you speaking, daughter?"

"To myself and my cloth," this time she lied to protect the bird, remembering what had happened when she told the truth before.

The Moon, feeling slightly guilty, thought to herself how her daughter must be actually losing her senses in reaction to the extreme isolation of her punishment.

Though exhausted and only vaguely interested, that evening when the Sun arrived from the bowels of Oblivion, hoping to sizzle off, eat, relax and sleep, he was forced again to listen as the long-haired Moon poured out the latest installment of her daughter's most recent antics. The Sun must have feared the Moon and dared not say, but considered the Moon's obsession with digging up more tales against their daughter to be a kind of laziness that came from both women having too much free time on their hands, unlike himself who only worked.

"She hasn't lost her memory of that strange short man at all," the jealous Moon reported, "rather she's losing her mind entirely, the neighbors said that they heard her ..." and so on until the Sun snored and the dark world shivered, waiting.

The day of the next dawning when the hummingbird squeezed in through the hole, he flew right to the Tall Girl and landed on her left thumb just below her opal thumbnail and sat there pert and at home. Holding the tiny, little, weighted, feathered jewel up to her breath, she spoke out her life and troubles as usual only this time when she spoke the little bird replied, "Yes, it has been dangerous and difficult, but at least we have one another, do we not?"

Weeping tears of confusion and grief and a strange form of joy, the Tall Girl recognized the voice of her short sweetheart long since fled, for whom she had suffered the punishment of the Gods. Then peering into his round, funny eyes she knew instantly that the hummingbird with the flashing banner tail of gold was none other than the Little Man himself.

"You know me now, don't you? I'm your sweetheart, the Short Boy whom your people seem to hate so much."

And wrapping him gently and easily in her fine copper hands she clasped him to her breasts then held him up to her big deer eyes, and eyeball to eyeball they began speaking the grand words again like they had in the past, taking up right where they'd left off, the Tall Girl with her beloved perched on her hand....

"When I saw you, I thought the Milky Way had dropped from the sky and got trapped in your eyes trying to crawl back to the skies." The little beast spoke to her well, his little feathered head twitching as he did. The girl laughed to see him scratch his head with his thread-like obsidian legs but replied through her smile, "In that endless dawn, in the time before the Sun, in the distance, I saw footprints that glowed in the dark in which the tears of night, like stars, had gathered. Following these tracks and by drinking the liquid from them, I survived and arrived at a campfire at whose edge I was made welcome. It was home I tracked and that footprint was made by you."

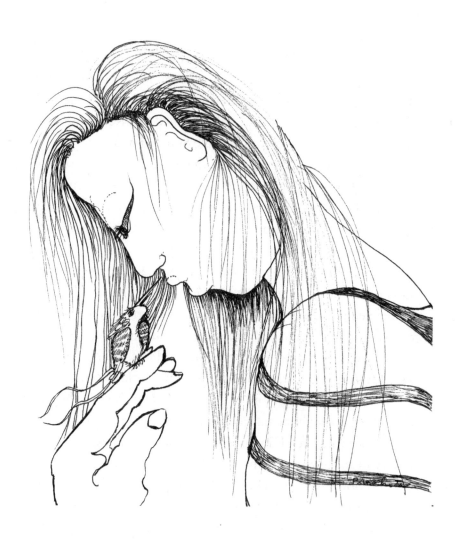

That's what they did all morning, noon and afternoon, the big, doe-skinned girl with eyes like pools gazing into the deep, tiny eyes of the flashing little bird that talked.

She didn't care what he looked like, whether he was big or small, animal or plant, rock or wind, after all, she was a Goddess; it was all the same to her. What mattered was that they loved each other and he hadn't gone away, he'd only changed forms in order to skip in undetected, past the scrutiny of the Sun and Moon.

So engrossed were they in each other's beauty that, like the time before, neither was on guard and had completely forgotten that the Grandmother Moon had begun returning early to listen to the girl speak to herself, in hopes of catching her in some delinquent activity or to determine the nature of her hysteria.

Today Grandmother Moon snuck up to the hut without the usual thuddings of her pumping feet and the normal abusive mutterings that seemed to accompany her tail-swishing arrival ever since she'd begun damming up the hut's doorway. Crouching outside beneath the rocky wall of the hut, the fierce old Goddess had been listening to the love prayers the girl made toward her little sweetheart.

Before the girl and the bird could do anything about it, the Moon had one fist through the matrix of the dammed up door, busting in fast in a surprise attack in hopes of seeing something to solve the mystery of the apparent happiness in the girl's voice.

In a motion well practiced and natural to all village girls who want to keep safe the little treasures they most cherish, the Tall Girl wrapped her fingers around her Little Birdman, tightening her grasp, then shoved the little fellow deep down into the ample folds of her *pót,* or Indian blouse, letting him loose, but hidden down by her sueded copper belly.

However, the little bird was still a bird and in the wild rushing instant of tumbling boulders and billowing dust through which the determined Moon stormed into the hut, he was forced by his nature to buzz around inside the beautiful girl's gown. He zoomed around her back and through and over her heavy luxurious breasts, up and down her ribs, tickling her with his wings everywhere the frenetic being chose to wander, all of which caused the girl to attempt to stop him by clasping her hand over where she thought he was, only to find he was too fast for her and had fled to a more sensitive spot, which caused her to laugh and grab more fervently in order to stop his tickling and keep him hidden from her jealous mother who now was just inside the threshold in a cloud of dust scowling in a fixed gaze at her insane daughter laughing and grabbing at her belly where Tall Girl had finally isolated the little bug-sized bird in a bubble of her magnificently woven blouse held gently with both of her smooth hands directly over her belly button.

"Are you ill, child?" spoke forth the tail-dragging Moon, now straddling the pile of jumbled stones.

"No, I'm fine," said her daughter with a frozen grin using all her will not to laugh or screech because the bird kept twitching her belly button, disobediently, causing it to tickle unbearably.

"Then why are you grabbing your belly? Do you have cramps?" the old lady asked squinting her eyes, sticking out her lips, pushing her jaw to one side and staring to the left for a short moment, as long as it took to express her contempt, during which, without her seeing, the hummingbird got loose inside the blouse again. This time Tall Girl had to laugh out loud while blurting out, "No. You quit that, my love." But before the Moon could return her gaze, the daughter, jumping like a fox on a rat, caught the bird on the move as he rounded the bend having flown the entire circumference of her waistline. By the time the Moon returned her disgusted gaze the girl was writhing on the earthen floor of the hut with uncontrollable hilarity, laughing with all her might and her hands still over her navel.

"Who are you speaking to and why are you holding your belly?" the old woman bellowed.

"I've been so lonely, mother, I decided to converse with my belly button, it talks just like my sweetheart but sometimes does not obey. I've seen yours, it really has a big smile; I guess as you get older your navel becomes more expressive." And then she let loose another peel of wild laughter as she stared at her stomach and hands which she then lifted to readjust her grip enough to stop the persistent bird without hurting him in her blouse.

Almost laughing out loud, so contagious was the sound, the Moon fought it back in the realization that her perfect daughter was now utterly deranged, having changed from a disobedient, adolescent princess to an unkempt lunatic who held conversations with her stomach.

Seeing that the Moon was fully convinced of her lunacy, the Tall Girl continued conversing with the hummingbird in whispers, while her mother went about her business in the compound. Subdued by her remorse, the Old Moon was even further convinced of her daughter's insanity listening to her mumble incessantly to her stomach. Her mother reckoned that the daughter, out of longing for an impossible thing, had been split like a log by the ax of her grief; one half of her was left laughing and chattering to her navel as if it were the boy she couldn't have, while the other half, her spirit, wandered lost somewhere unknown to the Moon.

A shaman, her brother-in-law, would have to be called the next day to find the girl's lost half, but until then she would do the girl's chores and pity her craziness.

When, overheated and in his usual huff, the Sun careened through the compound opening into his palatial grounds, the Moon was all over him with the news of their daughter's loss of reason.

But while the Moon felt the little hair of remorse that tickled her heart grow into a true flowering guilt, the Sun was too hot to care that they might have pushed their own perfect daughter too far and only wanted food and sleep.

The world was his concern and without his regularity would cease to be, and this thread of chaos that the Moon jerked and kept aroused did not help the Sun stay on course, and so the Sun blamed the Moon for his daughter's interruption of his routine. The Sun hated the Moon's changeable attitude and therefore resented her remorse. It was all crazy, irregular and useless. It should all go as demanded, but he had to deal with the strangeness of his compound's women; for a sleepless night was all he got, having to hear his daughter mumbling incessantly to her stomach, looking down her blouse throughout the night, while the guilty Moon wept every time her daughter laughed or spoke or made a gesture.

"Hee, hee," the tickled girl laughed.

"See, see, there she goes again," the Moon whispered to the Sun, who rolled his eyeballs. "We'll send for my sister's husband, the diviner, in the morning, won't we husband?" And elbowing the beleaguered Sun in his ribs, she forced the Sun to agree, although he did so in hopes all the chatter and commotion would calm down and he could rest for morning. Finally the Moon drifted off, and the Sun, who went to bed hungry though enraged, fell asleep to the rhythm of his wife's snoring and the bubbling stream of his daughter's whispering down her blouse.

When the world was deep in sleep, the hummingbird himself began to speak. Quietly to his sweetheart he said, "Tomorrow, we had better make a run for my village. I think we have to escape and go live awhile in my mother's house. If your mother, the Moon up in the sky, calls in a shaman, they will discover me, and the Moon will force your father to destroy me once and for all."

"It's true, this home is no longer friendly and my own thoughts are thought out for me, but where is your mother's house and who are your people?"

"I come from the sea, my mother is the great, driving, salty Woman Ocean who will love you and embrace you as she does me.

The flash and colors on my back I get from her. My father is the Lightning Fish, the Whale, the Water Deer, lord of Hurricane and he lives in the ocean. My mother's realm is even greater and older than your father's, but I didn't tell you because I wanted to love you as myself, and for you to want me for myself, instead of as our parents' namesakes. I'm one of the three brothers of the southern wind, who drive the life-giving rain that comes from the ocean onto your parent's land.

"If we flee together to the ocean and put but one of our toes into its brine, then all our troubles will be over. When we wet our feet in the sea, we will no longer be in the Sun's domain but in my mother's, and my family will protect us, for in her territory the Sun has no command or capacity to do us any harm.

"Protected by the powers of that great water, my parents shall give us good houses, food and help in my village until they can send gifts and speech-makers to your parents to heal the rift they might perceive we occur by our eloping. In the end all will be well. However, if we don't leave here, I'm afraid the Sun will not permit me to live, for knowing you now as intimately as I do, I would be executed, without a doubt. If we wet but one of your toes in my mother's sea, we are safe."

After a great deal of talk the girl agreed, pointing out that to facilitate their escape she had woven two knotted shoulder-capes that would make them invisible to the Sun who would otherwise surely see them as they moved the seventy miles to the sea.

As everybody expected, as soon as Sun Father had drifted, unfed, up the hill of the sky, the Moon set out in search of diviners and a shaman to fix her daughter's imperfection and strange behavior. But in her consternation she had neglected to close up the doorway, making it easy for the couple to make their escape. They must do it now, for if the Moon returned with a shaman, all would be lost.

To make this kind of decision, the Tall Girl should have been allowed a year to consider, for she would now be leaving her family and all she'd ever known and served, to follow her misunderstood heart and probably start a feud. No one would understand how she could follow this tiny, shiny fluff-ball to live in a land of infinite water where she would know nothing and perhaps live as an outsider, like the Shortman did in her village. But she did not have a year, a day or a morning to consider, and in the given situation, the desperate escalation of her parents' reactionary thinking and clannish, warlike stance made the moment dangerous and demanded from her that a choice be made.

She'd made her decision to leave, and in the frenzy to make their escape before the Grandmother Moon returned, the hummingbird became a man again, a short, shiny man with beautiful ears that would listen.

Tall Girl showed him what to pack, taking only the minimal, treasured appurtenances that sad, eloping girls have always calculated long before the eventuality becomes a fact, tying them into two thick, highly ornamented carrying cloths, *tqaqu* . She lifted one up onto her beautiful head, her elegant neck stretching to accommodate the weight, while the boy tied the other over his forehead, like a tumpline pack.

After unrolling the two invisibility capes, the Tall Girl knotted one around her Shortboy and tied herself into the other. A great shining world shone where once had stood two lovers. The magic clothes overwhelmed the sight of any viewer with the devastating beauty of the natural world the girl had woven into them, in which moving animals, moving windy trees, creeping clouds, yawning animals and lazy stones were all alive and each proceeding according to its nature.

And in all this the boy and girl, as unique and particular beings, were utterly buried, lost in the complex foment and beauty of the world they now wore upon their backs. Thus hidden they trotted off unnoticed toward the distant Ocean whose eyebrows of sea foam crashed, to the kingdom of Hurricane, away from the girl's beloved homeland and the Village of the Sun and Moon.

Those things she'd decided to bring along grew heavier the farther they traveled. The Tall Beauty and her Hummingbird Boy, inspired by their love for each other, driven by the fear of having it taken away, pushed even harder toward the coast. They trotted up hills, down the zig-zag trails of deep ravines, over ridges, along ridges, under tumbled boulders, over fallen trees, through thickets, briars, dense forests, down a stream bed, into a dry riverbed that cut directly through the coastal savanna and all the intricacies of land that separated the Mountain Domain of the Moon and the Sun from the infinite rippling curved plains of turquoise salty water called Ocean.

The beautiful daughter of the Sun made rhythms with her stride, forcing her serpent-skin skirts to whistle as they rustled like a wind right behind the bobbing movement of her sweetheart, who knew the path all too well for having traveled it daily when they were still courting.

Though their journey was otherwise unhindered and proceeded unperceived by any who would have curtailed it, as expected, the girl's absence was soon discovered. The Moon returned to the hut with a good diviner to find that her daughter and her clothing were missing, and knowing not what to think, began to think it all. Had her girl wandered off in her lunacy, perhaps drowning in the lake or falling and cracking her head upon a stone? Had she been kidnapped? Was she simply visiting her aunties and telling terrible tales about her mother? "Who could say?" she muttered.

Of course the diviner could have easily solved the riddle, but the royal hysteria of the anxious Moon made the subject impossible to broach. Too frantic to sit down to make a calm divination anymore, the long-haired, crazed Moon dashed around the village, along the shore of the lake, crying out, but finding no sign of the girl, ran up the Mountain of the Sky to notify the Sun.

Searching the Earth from the highest point in the sky with his far-seeing eyes and not finding his beautiful daughter, the Sun, as the Moon had demanded, called out the guard. Every one of his brothers, the Gods that ran the sky, came rushing in when the Sun blasted and puffed the bugled code on his long, wooden warrior horn, like those that rested on the top of every mountain long ago.

Nabey al lightning came, *Roxal* lightning, *Rucabal* lightning came, *Chp* lightning came, *Sac* lightning came, *Qan* lightning, *Ciac* lightning came, Whirlwind lightning came, all of them came until all twelve had arrived including hateful *Q iq ,* to make thirteen brothers with their older brother the Sun.

The Sun, who couldn't leave his sky road, made his case to his brothers, petitioning them to course the earth in search of the Beautiful Girl, since nobody could tell what had become of her.

As each of the weather Gods unfurled their flying capes and armed up for the search, Q iq elbowed his way to the center of the throng and, holding them back, blew his hard, infertile wind down and across the southern coast just a couple of miles shy of the wild strand of black volcanic sand at the edge of the Sun's Mountain Earth. Toward where the white eyelashes of the Grandmother Ocean surf blinked and rumbled, Q iq blew his cold, unhappy wind, getting underneath the capes of invisibility that kept the boy and girl even from the sight of the Sun, and tossing them up over their heads, exposed the couple's rushing movement to full view of all the world, especially the sky Gods who stood there gaping with the Sun. All the brothers breathed easier, thinking all was well, that the girl had been found alive, that Q iq had generously, mysteriously, uncharacteristically succeeded where they had not.

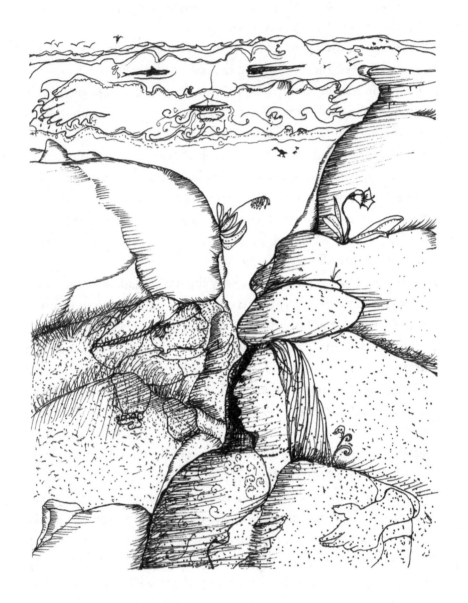

The powerful lord of Whirlwind Thunder stepped forward and grabbed his stunned old brother's arm, speaking to the Sun in a relieved tone, "Hey, look, your Beautiful Daughter isn't lost; she's fallen in love with the son of the Ocean and is running away to live there in the palace of the Hurricane. You can bet if they get there, there will be a big feast. I hope we get invited."

The Sun almost speechless in his fury roared back at his brother, "What are you saying, you mean to tell me that this lowlife is the son of Hurricane?"

"*Jieach* , yes, man," all his brothers proudly chimed together, each of them grinning and happy, all except hateful Q iq who looked disgusted with the whole scene.

"If he gets just one hair in there," said the Whirlwind, meaning the Ocean, "we'd be powerless to take her back anyway."

As the Gods spoke, the lovers came within a couple of hundred yards of the Old Lady Sea who was beckoning to them now to hurry. The girl's father knew full well that if he jumped to the Earth in his present heated form to ferry his daughter back to his home, he would cause the entire Earth to burst into flame, kill all of creation, ruin Time itself for leaving his routine and path and only vaporize his daughter in the process.

Blustering and frustrated and feeling helpless, dishonored and with his authority thwarted, the haughty Sun addressed his warrior brothers.

"Go. Get her back, now. Brothers, use your specific powers each according to his ability. If I could leave the sky, I'd do it myself. We shouldn't care what happens to that fool boy. Just bring back my daughter in one piece. Kill the boy if you must to accomplish it. But let my daughter come back unscathed, don't hurt her."

Hemming and hawing, looking off in all directions but the Sun's, the powerfully built Sky Gods waffled a bit. Shrugging their shoulders and looking at their feet like men around a hole, none of them were immediately prepared to throw thunderbolts and interfere with their niece's love without proper deliberation.

Whirlwind again spoke first to the Sun, "Brother, look there. They're just children. Kids in love. Don't you remember how it was for you and the Moon, long ago?"

Like the entire creation, the Sky Gods loved their niece and thought as Hummingbird had hoped they would, that they should wait and negotiate later with Ocean and Hurricane, when things settled down, at least to keep the peace on the Earth and in that way allow their wonderful niece to follow the love of her heart.

All the while the couple trotted, ran, panted, trotted, trotted and trotted and with their young chests heaving and sweating they could hear all along the call of the boy's Ocean Mother calling to her future daughter-in-law to hurry in a voice of gentle surf.

"*Ktjo aii,* come on you two,

Ktjo aii, alnaq ga, come here you two, hurry,

Alnaq ga, hurry,

Xin pet adta, rival chawa, your father's bunch are on their way, he bears a grudge against you,

Rival nuban, he stirs a grudge within him,

Ktjo yaan al naq yaxtan, come to me little daughter, hurry miss girl,

Wal ala, my baby boy, come."

And by now the Beautiful Girl and Shiny Little Man were within ten feet of the Ocean, who was reaching out toward them in great waves of longing to touch them both and take them home safe on the back of the Water Deer, the lightning fish, the whales.

Caught in the confusion of a desperate moment's decision, the Sun again ordered his brothers to stop the boy at any cost because he would not lose his daughter to a little man who had acted so dishonorably....

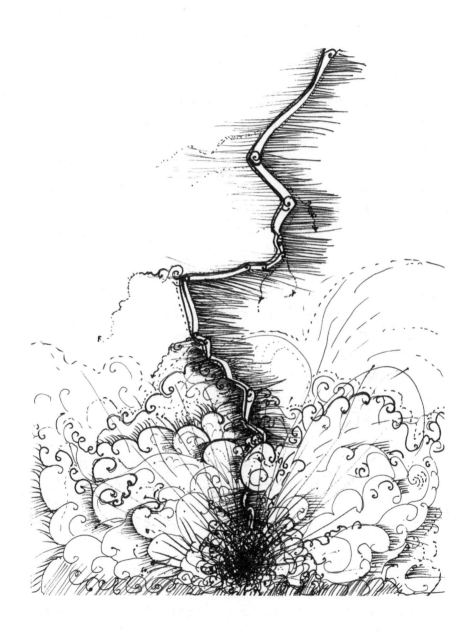

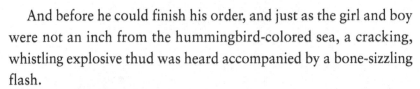

And before he could finish his order, and just as the girl and boy were not an inch from the hummingbird-colored sea, a cracking, whistling explosive thud was heard accompanied by a bone-sizzling flash.

The stench of lightning ozone permeated the air along that great beach which still glowed phosphorescent through the thick, nauseating smoke of the lightning blast, blurring the sight of all in the long silence that followed.

Never having reached his mother's waters, Hummingbird Boy had been stunned and tossed unconscious down the black sand beach by the blast like a blown leaf.

He awoke to a world in tears. Every stone was weeping, his mother kept murmuring over and over, *"Natzraga? Natzraga?"* Why? Why? Why? weeping all the while. The trees were weeping, the sky was weeping, the animals wept. The entire world and everything in it wept; for when the smoke had cleared and the boy had regained his legs, he went to search, calling out for his sweetheart, the Tall Girl.

When he found her, the Daughter of the Sun was in pieces, thrown about the world in the most powerfully rude and casual way from the blast, which had hit her square. Her beautiful head could see no more, nor speak one life-giving word. The Tall Girl's heart had been blown completely out of her chest, sailing far down the beach to rest, half buried in the hot beach sand and there ceased to beat. One of her wonderful hands was over there, and a foot on the other side of that; scattered everywhere, she was now spread out in bits throughout the grieving earth.

Q iq hated the Sun for his beautiful daughter. He hated Hummingbird Boy for the love she bore him. Q iq hated his brothers for their jolliness and the love they had for the girl and he hated the world as it was. He wanted the Ocean to hate the Sky, to start a war that would end it all.

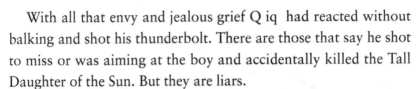

With all that envy and jealous grief Q iq had reacted without balking and shot his thunderbolt. There are those that say he shot to miss or was aiming at the boy and accidentally killed the Tall Daughter of the Sun. But they are liars.

Q iq deliberately blew her to pieces to take away what the world loved, to make the creation suffer just what he suffered when the world wouldn't love him. He killed her; then like the excellent wind he was, he fled back to his nest on the other side of Oblivion, where he lives today, from which he pays us frequent visits.

Cradling her great smooth heart in his arms, the Shortboy, son of Hurricane and the Ocean, fell screaming to his knees on that sparkling beach. He rocked and sobbed out all the tears of the world, all the water of the Earth onto her heart, howling in the deepest imaginable grief, disgusted with disbelief over the possessive arrogance of her parents. He cursed his slowness and roared his hatred of the Sky, pounding the sand so long and hard it was reduced to the fineness of talc.

Not one thing held back, and nothing was exempted, but all the world ceased to try, weeping beyond the limits. What had made the world live seemed now entirely defeated.

All this weeping of the world continued for longer than people today have ways to measure and beyond our imaginations and plunged the world into a sea of dust and dying plants, a drought of final proportions that took hold throughout, for all the water was wept out and into the Ocean, and none was left upon the land.

For when the Daughter of the Sun was dismembered, she left the world without its flowering or its moisture.

For without her the world refused to grow, Time ceased to be a countable thing, a day could have been a century, a minute an hour, and Hummingbird spent thousands of uncountable years rolled up like a sowbug on the beach, bound there as a sacrifice to his longing by his lost love, sorrowfully whimpering and pouring tears onto the heart of his beloved which he clutched inextractably in his salt-encrusted arms.

After another thousand timeless years, Hummingbird Boy spent the next millennium dragging himself to his feet, thinking to return with her heart to the bottom of his Ocean homeland. He would start a war against the Sky and hope to be killed right out. But the longer he stood holding her heart, the more a certain thought began to surface in the bubbling pot of his thinking where the conflicting possibilities for the remainder of his useless life stewed. Since his birth from the great fish-filled womb of the Ocean, Hummingbird Boy had always been fated for and pointed toward a life spent as a diviner and a shaman, and it was this glimmer of natural strangeness that had made him shine. But that shine had now been rewired, amplified and deeply set in motion by the same stunning blast that had taken from him his only reason to live. The boy that had loved the girl had died as well in the lightning, and a new man grew out of the three-thousand-year grief and whimpering sleep that followed. With all that and nothing left to lose, Hummingbird now remembered in his bones an Ocean thought, an ancient song, a jumping-bones-back-together ritual way of doing, a raising up of plants, bringing-back-water-way, and in the churning foment of all those forgotten things remembered, the man climbed onto the back of a different kind of love and rode its possibility toward the doing of something most likely impossible. Telling no one of his intentions, Hummingbird Boy took to gathering together all the pieces of his beautiful friend, the pieces of the girl, the pieces of his dead Goddess, the Daughter of the Sun and Moon.

Placing every particle of his beloved on top of one another, one by one, each wrapped in the particular leaf from the tree or plant under which it had been thrown, the Hummingbird packed all of them in turn into a great *yaal* or string net bag whose knots were made of stars, and tied it all down secure and tight with her heart still clutched to his chest.

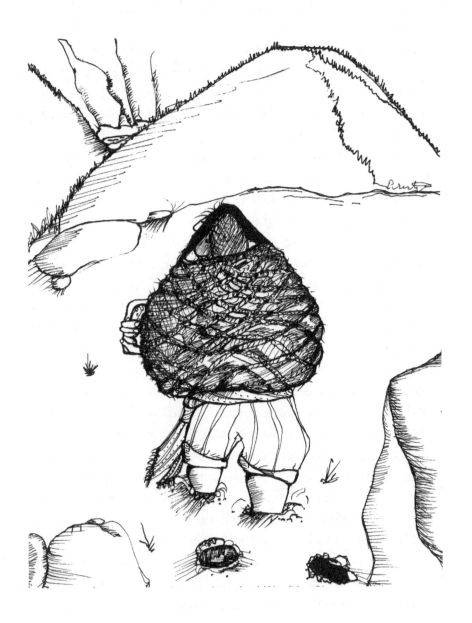

By standing up with a tumpline attached to his pack that ran over his more furrowed forehead, Hummingbird Man hoisted her remains upon his back.

Thus hitched beneath the dead memory of her, he trudged off to deliver her body to her people in the Village of the Sun. He backtracked through every river course, gorge and gully, cinder mountain, thicket, bog and stream, up and up and over the hills and ridges, retracing every step he'd taken with her, under whose remains he now sweated. She was heavy in her death, heavier than most could have managed. So heavy in fact that Hummingbird Man sank into the earth up to his hips with every step he took, and in this way struggled on until he got there.

He didn't need to hide this time for if they killed him as well, it wouldn't matter, but because he didn't hide, when he arrived, the whole world was there waiting for him.

Though the crowd was miles deep with every being of this creation pressing and craning their necks to get a glimpse of what they had all loved and lost, they hung their heads and courteously parted, wept the waterless tears of their droughted hearts and gave way and access to the royal compound of the tall and once shining parents of his dead sweetheart, the Sun and the Moon, who stood facing the now silent throng, heads hung with shame and horror, unable to look the Hummingbird in the face.

And in the silence of a million breathing beings holding their breaths, Hummingbird Boy, like a returning hunter, let down his load, swinging her flesh gently back to her village earth.

It was all finished and there he left her. Having completed what he'd promised himself, Hummingbird Man turned to leave, but half way, spun back around and addressed the Sun and Moon.

"I thought to bring your daughter back, the one you killed because you only wanted tall son-in-laws from the sky, because you didn't want short, unknown, unseen beings; you wouldn't let

her love the small and make the world flower. She is now dismembered because of your jealousy and tribalist stupidities. The
love all of us felt for her should have been sufficient to have kept
her together. But it was not.

"So, here she is, the child of your thinking, dismembered, and
in pieces, she will now agree to your every whim.

"This is your work."

Then as the entire world, the village crowd, the Gods and all
those assembled there let rise an earth-splitting wail of grief and
shame, Hummingbird knelt to kiss her remains, and backing up a
few steps, turned and walked in a tired pace toward the Ocean,
unburdened now, but empty.

The grief-stricken crowds followed him chattering, impeding his
direction, until the Moon herself, having broken the line, came running
after him, her disheveled white hair matted and trailing in the dust of
the drought. The old woman fell to her knees weeping, almost tack-
ling him as she locked her powerful arms around his standing knees.

Speaking through her heart-rending sobs, the Moon begged over
and over again for his forgiveness, explaining repeatedly how they
all realized how really wrong they all had been, how the Gods were
wrong.

Walking out of her grasp, still enraged by this too convenient,
late admission of guilt with no recognition of the cause for what so
easily could have been prevented, without looking down at her nor
back, the Hummingbird continued on his journey home to the Ocean.

Capturing him again, she pleaded in a different tone, "Son-
in-law, you who turned yourself into a little green *Tzunuun*,
Hummingbird, then back into a boy and then into the sparkling
child of Ocean, is there any truth in what I see is your great ability
with magic to restore my daughter back to life? Is there nothing you
can do or heard tell or seen performed, some song or method that
could cause my daughter's face to return again? Could you bring

her back to life? I so long to see her again. A magician you are and a great shaman I think. I plead with you, make an attempt of any kind to bring her back, if you can."

"If there were anything I could have done alone to see my beloved's copper sueded face again, don't you think I would have done so already? What I myself wouldn't give to see her again either as she was when we had to hide from you or as what she might become today. If I knew a way, I would be there now floating drowned in the pools of her eyes, and the world should be a moist home to revived plants and animals. But here we are in this hopeless, dry flatness with what we love still dismembered.

"Yet Grandmother Moon, what I will tell you is the following: When this world had not yet fruited, been born or set into motion, there were ways I can remember for reasons beyond the telling by which a body, dismembered in just such a way as my love and your daughter, could be revived. It is highly unlikely that the likes of you and I could ever make such a thing happen, but if we wanted to try, I'm willing, if you are.

"I say, if you are willing, for the one and only chance by which it might work to bring your daughter alive is if you are willing to obey everything I say to you and cause the world to obey my demands. We would have to use our powers together but only under my direction. Hummingbird Man, the Short Man, child of Ocean and Hurricane, would have to be the boss."

Considering the nature of the Moon and the autocratic way she had always carried on, this would be a hard and doubtful change. Without balking, knowing now that she loved her daughter more than she loved her hate of anyone telling her what to do, she replied, "What do you need from me, son?"

"The first thing you must do if we succeed in bringing life back to her poor separated body is to agree to fully accept her however she appears. What do you say?"

"Of course, I promise, this time to accept her as she will be."

"Second, if she comes back alive, you will allow her to marry me if she agrees to it?" With her face toward the earth, the Moon agreed to this as well.

The enormous crowd, expectant, thrilled and mollified, opened up as the boy motioned for them to make a space for him to work, after which he made his first demand.

"Bring me a big sacrificial cooking pot, a new, well-cured, hard-fired *p'tish* with a large mouth."

This was duly fetched and offered to the man by some friend of the dead girl.

"Now as a cover, bring me a tree-gourd, a *tzimai.*"

An old man brought one that the Hummingbird expertly split exactly in half, scraping out the seed pulp, which he scattered to the crowd.

"Put the pot under the Moon's fancy raised balsa wood bed, please."

Five married women carried it and gently situated the beautiful hard-fired, red, earth pot with the burgundy-colored fire mark onto a *yagual,* a *sotoy* ring right where the shaman directed beneath the bed of the Moon.

Lighting a fire with the small mirror hummingbirds have on their chests, the man incensed the pot inside and out as well as the Moon herself and finally the four corner posts of the bed, which he called legs and feet, mountain and sky thrones. Then he called for more.

"Now bring me leaves of the *maxan* plant still fresh in this drought."

"Now bring me the leaves of the *pixc* tree."

"Now bring me the leaves of the wild red *tzub tzub* banana."

"Now bring the leaves of the *chaj.*"

"Now bring me leaves of the *c'siis.*"

"Now bring me leaves of *tzejtel.*"

"Now bring me leaves of *kixlan che*."
"Now bring me leaves of *oj*."
"Now bring me leaves of *kxub*."
"Now bring me leaves of *kinoum*."
"Now bring me leaves of *quash*."
"Now bring me leaves of *kím*."
"Now bring me leaves of *kiip* ."

Every time he called out for leaves, the Moon would point to some bystanders, and they would eagerly depart for the wilds surrounding the Village of the Sun, their bare feet thudding like herds of wild peccaries rushing past, returning sometimes hours later out of breath in the same thundering dedication. And as the leaves arrived cradled in bunches in the arms of one or more of the helpful and excited villagers, his body rocking, his head rolling, tears falling, the shaman, Hummingbird Boy sang a series of old secret songs and *kilaj tzij* , delicious prayer words, while wrapping each specific part of the girl's body in a different plant. Then one at a time he placed each little package carefully into the smoking pot, changing the song for each piece as they piled and layered toward the opening.

First he put inside what had been her feet,
And then what was once her calves,
And then her thighs,
Then the trunk and ribs and back and spine,
And then the arms,
Then the forearms,
And her beautiful hands.

On top of all the rest he made a nest of *kím*, a sweet, tall grass from the volcanoes, and placed her poor head in the pot like an egg. Covering that with a layer of corn leaves, he put the heart in last, which he'd wrapped with a little of every one of all the leaves he'd called for plus a tuft of his own top-knot feathers and bound it all into a package using thirteen strands of the Moon's long white hair as cordage.

Finally the Hummingbird took one of the halves of the split tree gourd and closed the opening of the pot with it, bowl side up.

Now standing, taking a breath, staring at the pot under the Moon's bed, Hummingbird began a tearful oration that lasted the entire day and night. Not until the following dusk did he leave off with his long prayer when he turned to the Moon.

"Grandmother, this pot is now an egg, your child has become its yolk and you are now a mother bird. You must hatch your daughter back to life. At night, as soon as the Sun sets, you must stay in your nest, remain in your bed, never leaving for any reason until the Sun rises again. While on the nest, you mustn't sleep either for then we shall fail. Under no conditions shall you open the pot beneath you or lift its lid. Above all do not open it no matter what sounds you hear coming from the pot. If you do, you shall not see your daughter as she was. Only I, the Hummingbird Man, will be the one to finally open the pot on the sunrise of the thirteenth day. Perhaps if you do this all well, on the thirteenth day you will see her face again.

"Every morning I will return at dawn to listen, sing and pray. The rest of the time, I will be in the mountain doing the work shamans do to make life live."

Aware of how little practice the Moon had in the art of following orders instead of giving them, the Hummingbird repeated it all several times to make certain that they understood each other. Then turning into a green hummingbird with a long iridescent tail, the shaman rocketed in a rolling motion into the wild mountain forest that waited south of the Village of the Sun.

As directed, the Tall Girl's mother climbed up on her squeaky balsa wood bed at dusk and lay there all night, awake, imagining her beloved child and how she might return just as she had been when she had left. This time the Moon wouldn't treat her daughter's thoughts and feeling with disdain, she could marry the crazy little Hummingbird Boy and the world could go on.

After her husband left the compound and the day began to dawn, the Moon was drifting into a slumber of dreams when a vibration of movement and a scratching like squirrels rustling through a pile of dried corn husks came faintly from the pot. Drunk on her grief-driven hope, the longing for her daughter's face, and the delirious daze of a sleepless night, this sign of life from the pot, the egg she was to hatch, drove the old lady wild. But still she waited until the Sun had risen, and sliding madly off her bench, she crouched down and put her ear as close as she might dare without actually touching any-thing and listened. When the thing inside the pot moved again and the whole hut sang with the sound, curiosity flooded her old bossy bones, and the Moon reached to lift the gourd to peek and see what her daughter had become, and the very instant as she was about to

do so, Hummingbird Boy jumped in through the doorway, and pulled her back just in time to cause their project to survive at least one more day.

The night that followed was quiet and the Moon kept a dedicated vigil, but at dawn the pot was making sounds again. So much so, that all the neighbors came around to stare. The pot was pinging and groaning as if it were cooking, albeit there was no flame beneath it. It sounded like it would boil over in a minute.

Just as the Moon, whose eyes were fixed in a glazed amazement, was reaching to lift the lid, Hummingbird, his feathers all crooked and his head all fluffy, skidded in through the doorway and rolled the Moon back on the ground just in time. The two of them lay on their backs panting for a spell.

"Don't you understand?" the Hummingbird Boy admonished. "If you had removed the gourd, your daughter would have been a pot of angry churning bees forever? Don't do that again, please."

But on the third dawn the pot began to hiss and rasp in a writhing fierceness which for some reason the reptile Moon felt might be her daughter and once again the indignant hummingbird arrived back from the mountains in barely time enough to pull the mother back from her insistent curiosity.

And it went the same way, every morning. Though every day, the longhaired Moon promised with her very soul that she would do better, she was never able to master her curiosity when it ran together with her grief. She had to possess everything and know everything. Aware of this, the Hummingbird Man always came just in time to keep the Moon from interrupting and destroying her daughter's daily changes and private transformations from one kind of beast, into a storm, into another kind of creature, into whatever unknown thing she had to become and so she was able to proceed relatively unhindered, although what was in the pot was always endangered by her mother, the Moon.

On the fourth dawn a sound of bony armor rattled the air.

On the fifth, the scuttling, snipping sounds of scorpions stung the pot.

Before the Sun rose on the sixth day a great watery splashing rocked the vessel.

And on the seventh, a squealing issued forth like an ocelot crushing a rabbit by the throat.

With the eighth morning came the gnashing teeth of peccaries.

Then by the ninth a little quiet panting sound, a squeak, some claws and then the wind.

The tenth dawn sounded all the world like ten billion bark borers chewing down a forest.

The eleventh, a plaintive drumming, like that from the throats of pie-billed grebes. And in every case the Moon almost ruined it all and the Hummingbird saved it.

On the twelfth, one day left, the hour growing nearer, the world shook with expectation and dread, and the Moon was more crazed than ever, so much so, that when the sound of that twelfth dawn rose up through her bed, the sleepless, wobbly Moon could not endure it anymore. For beneath her from the twelfth-day-pot rose a human voice, a breathy cooing sound like a teenage girl moaning over and over in ecstasy, and upon hearing a girl's voice, she supposed it was her daughter's. Euphoric and impatient, the Moon slithered off her bed and lifted the gourd clear off the pot over which she was to sit hatching for just one more day.

Hummingbird blew into the hut just a millisecond too late to stop the hope-crazed woman from prematurely opening the pot. Though the beautiful and unabashed moaning continued throughout, nothing of a girl came out of the pot.

"Listen, boy," her unkempt white hair and crazy head trembling as she spoke, "It's her voice, you know it well, don't you. It's her all right. I can't believe it; you did it. It's her. How do we get her out of that pot?"

Pulling the old woman to her feet and moving her to stand behind him where the crowds of villagers had gathered thick, the boy took four neighbors and pulled the twelve-day-pot out from beneath the balsa bed of the Moon into the light of day, into the courtyard of the Sun.

And it was there that the boy began to chant his old courting love poems to the hard-fired, red, clay pot with the burgundy fire mark on its side:

"When I saw you I thought the Moon
had drunk too much at the feast
and fell out of the sky
and went tottering around the village
looking for home.
But I was mistaken,
it was the glowing ember in your head
that emerged looking for a welcome,
please, Tall Girl,
come sit by my fire.
When I saw you ..."

And as he went on and on speaking the old praise poems with which Tall Girl and he had dazzled each other long before, a little soft and blunt ruby-colored horn emerged from the pot, covered in iridescent feathers. Then it receded and rose up again, only this time it was attached to the top of a big curly feathered head of a gorgeous, shimmering, black bird bigger than a wild oscellated turkey. She had yellow legs and a long, wide, black tail through which an immaculate ivory band, a palm's width stretched across, half way up. When fully emerged from her earthenware egg, which hummingbird had carefully cracked with a stone, this never-before-seen-bird strutted on one yellow foot at a time while the other folded beneath her at every step.

When every so often she let out a cry, that same ecstatic moan that had come from the pot, it was the same wild moan we hear in the mountains in the late spring when the rains return after the long dry season, the sound of the shy *ciac tunuun,* or horned guan.

Turning to the Moon, Hummingbird Boy, the son of Ocean and Hurricane, spoke:

"This is the daughter that your uncontrollable curiosity and the impatience of your envy has chosen, but to me she is as beautiful as ever in her new form, and I take her for my wife." And turning himself into a hummingbird for the last time, he hovered up at eye level with the new bird, and they gazed into each other's wild, round eyes.

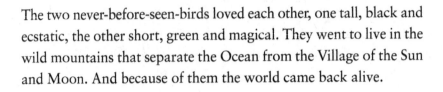

The two never-before-seen-birds loved each other, one tall, black and ecstatic, the other short, green and magical. They went to live in the wild mountains that separate the Ocean from the Village of the Sun and Moon. And because of them the world came back alive.

Five Layers of Understandings of the Story

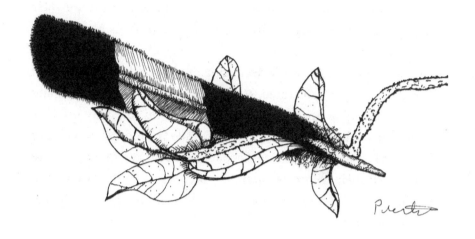

First Layer: Iridescent Tail Feathers

The Outer Wrappings of the Story

How many of our fathers had fathers like the Sun? And how many of them grew up to become fathers just like the Sun, fathers who couldn't see us and who took us for granted while immersing all their waking hours into a hard job that, although it did keep the world of the family alive and together, kept him away from the family? All powerful in his own world and powerless outside it, he would spend all his male fire on that limited world, which to his small children was the whole world, only to return home over-heated, exhausted, cutting everything and everybody down with what the Mayans call the "sharp teeth of our father," referring to the hot rays of the Sun father.

How many working women and men in this age had parents who taught them that praise was unimportant and never to be expected, and in order to hide the natural grief such men and women feel at this culturally endorsed absence of sincere praise for their impossible jobs have trivialized their own emotions as frivolous extravagances of the mind?

If a culture doesn't know well enough to pour the daily water of welcome over the frustrated, overworked heads of these men and women returning home from a big, hard world that may not love them, then is it any wonder that they hide behind the newspaper hoping to escape further into sleep and dreams, the quicker to rise away from their failure as parents to become again the distant and heroic Gods the family thinks they are and about which the bigger world knows nothing?

How many men and women have no one to "sizzle" them down, to mop them off, feed them and listen to their daily story in order to cool them off from the hard, draining heights they travel all day, and who end up by pouring the liquid liquor of fiery resentment inside of them to numb their grief instead of the cooling water of recognition over their tired heads?

Are there still teenage girls in this world who have mothers just like the Moon? Mothers who were proud, sane and friendly while their daughters were little girls, but upon the appearance of the young lady's swelling breasts, beautiful eyes, changing skin and curvaceous hips, became overnight unreasonable, vicious, reptilian, anxiety-ridden trolls who would now "keep the order," so possessive of their children as to think of their daughter's charm and ability as their own personal creations?

When she was a child, was the Moon, or any of our mothers, anything like the Tall Girl, who like many of us, totally in love with our parents at an early age, and as dutiful and hopeful youngsters lived only for a rare compliment from our overbusy parents, sure as we were that the reason our parents did so many unknowable things that kept them away was because they were dedicated to keeping the Sun and the Moon in the sky? We thought the entire world depended on our parents, and as little people we felt a great responsibility to do our part by helping them in all we did, supplying our parents with our little clannish loyalties to aid a cause we didn't fully comprehend.

The story seems to say, as every Mayan story does, that all of this is part of life and will happen in all people's lives in one form or the next, and lacking that in this synthetic age, the rest of the story cannot be lived out. This is not to say that we should try to be like the beings in the story, it just means that by nature we are like the beings in the story, and no matter how much we attempt to adjust our realities to avoid suffering, a certain quota of suffering is inevitable. But there is suffering that causes beauty and can lead to a life well lived, and then there is suffering that causes more suffering.

Though it forms only the wrapper in which the deeper indigenous layer of the story hibernates, this outer layer of the story is valuable on a personal level for modern people not only for itself. Just as iridescent feathers molted from the tail of a rare jungle bird when found on the trail are not the actual bird, though beautiful in and of themselves, tell us that the magical bird is around somewhere, so the deeper magic of the story lies waiting under this first layer to draw us away from the confusing quagmire of the concerns of commercial culture into the forest of the Indigenous Soul.

This layer of the story then is about what it takes and what happens for any of us as a young person when we attempt to escape the once grand universe of what is now the too limited reality of our family clan, neighborhood, town, school, culture or race, for which we maintain a deep, nostalgic affection, in order to follow what we love with our natural born uniqueness.

Though separation from our families and their way of life has been broadly proclaimed as a major characteristic of becoming an adult and finding one's individuality, the story seems to say our initiation into a useful human form comes not from what we are given, but from the difficulties we are forced to negotiate that always arise when we, from a place of grief and desire, finally follow that shiny thing we love toward the great pulsing unknown.

No matter what, as children we start out as short beings. For all children, every adult is a giant, and their parents are Gods whose faces hang overhead in the upper regions of their young worlds. In actuality, standing upon the solid Holy Earth, looking up from the eye level of our parents' knees, the sky is not so much farther than the ceiling in our family's house, and from where they look down to us, the sky's moon and the sun seem to merge with our parents' faces.

It is a long way up there to where the Sun and Moon, our parents, spend their days, but they come down to visit us and sometimes carry us flying through the sky, with us giggling and euphoric, proud to be their only children.

If we have proud parents, tribalist parents, successful people for parents, parents proud of their own origins and proud of us as their children as extensions of their ancestral pride, then it could be, like Tall Girl, that we are consistently reminded of how immense we must learn to become in order to be the living representatives of such grandness. Treated as something that big, we believe we are that big. As each parent has been raised to know their personal lineage is greater than their spouse's line, the combination of the two must be in their literalist minds greater than either. By the time we reach puberty at an age where the ability to make new additions to the dynasty begins to push us into flower and desire, we have outgrown even ourselves, when our parents add our personal excellence, abilities, pride and beauty onto the height of their own origins. In this time-honored type of tribal bind, for the parents to see themselves as tall and grand, they must have children who are taller and grander still.

But these are lonely children grown so tall that no one can reach them. They are brought into this world astride a gigantic monster horse of ancestral history so overwhelmingly large that the young person's own subtle shape and unique abilities appear as small and indistinguishable parts of the creature's own mountainous bulk. Though the world around sees the creature and the child on top it as just the child itself, from the withers of this ancestral monster, the child sees the world in a magnificent overview, but from a height where any particular thing is much too small and far away for either to embrace. To become an individual means to fall in love with the beauty of one of these small faraway things inside the grandeur of it all. Though we might be trampled or exiled in our attempt, we must find the courage and personal ingenuity to invent a way down off that beast to be with what we love.

Nowdays in places where television, advertising and media have taken the place of what used to be the tribal voice of the parent, we find ourselves riding a synthetic monster of equal height who has devoured the old monster of ancestral weight. On the backs of this artificial behemoth both children and parents are held hostage, remaining the same size as the kids, told by the voice what to want and how to look, duping us into thinking that we are already big individuals and can remain young and tall by conforming to the appearances of such a soulless, unimaginative daydream, never realizing that the unnatural culture generated by obeying the sarcastic voice of the monster is the house of a vicious, devouring, self-important parent. All of us in today's culture should do our best to act when we fall in love with something small and real and climb back to the earth, escaping the living death of synthetic modernity by following the beautiful, small, shiny, diligent thing that could cause us to find our true shape and keep the world's diversity of possibility alive.

Few children, however, are praised so much as to be made so tall by their parents. Like Short Boy in the story, these children will probably revere the tall, celebrated, untouchable thing as much as Tall Girl must love the small.

All people need to be praised, but the praise should only be spent on what is praiseworthy. The encouragement of praise must be given to all people, especially our youth, who should be praised for *their* ability to praise the magnificence around them. To be praised, one must first learn how to praise.

That is what the Short Boy and Tall Girl do when they meet: they are not being praised, they are praising each other. True praise is not something that raises people away from the earth they must finally rest in; praise is a grief-soaked type of life-endorsing way of speaking that brings the praised closer to the world that is otherwise so hard to live in. Praise does not make haughty, it brings life. Anything else is an empty seduction that makes words into things that are lesser than they should be.

And yet the story tells us that even real praise is not enough to cause our individuality to happen. Our individuality does not come from our successes as perceived by tribe, family or culture, but rather on how we wrestle and dance with our failures after life makes us short, flattens us and pulls us into pieces and usually without the endorsement of our upbringing.

As a devoted child, the Tall Girl, like many of us at first, instead of rebelling or running away believes the family rhetoric that the world will end if she lowers herself from the large, tall, sky-born to the low, subtle earth-born. She becomes neurotically devoted to the everyday details of oppressive thinking that keep her away from the great teeming world and any possibility of finding her uniqueness. Anyone who has done this and not escaped will most likely be unable to tell us how easily a whole lifetime can be spent missionizing on behalf of what is killing them, while attending to its every need.

On the other hand, for a person destined to become a beauty-making person, a truly alive person, the great isolating height enforced upon us by the family or the culture may not always have sufficient power to keep us from our excellence despite the impossible, banal conditions imposed upon our hopeful spirits.

Like the Tall Girl's forbidden love for the Short Boy, what is truly substantial in us begins to find its heart's desire in "small," beautiful, easy-to-hide things.

This smallness helps to keep one's desire hidden and makes it possible that the subtle understanding and true feelings of a young person might be protected, going unnoticed by a society who would have us loving only the big, the obvious, the sensational, the taxable, the literal and acceptable.

If the youth only love what they are told to love by their parents or their parent's culture through designer anxieties thrown at them by television and advertising tailored to sell them appearances and stuff to cure the panic set loose in their scared young bodies by the same, then the culture either directly or implicitly is telling youth that the unique things they love are something "beneath them," unimpressive, overly organic, messy, unprofitable or small. It is no marvel then that we are actually teaching our children to hide their love, if only because the young people might fear that the magic in the object of their affections will be trivialized, crushed, or co-opted by their parents, like the Moon does to Tall Girl.

If parents are not courageous enough to corroborate the true beauty their children see when they see it and to allow the youth to keep it as their own, or there are not mentors outside the family to counter this kind of ignorance, then like the Moon they will force their children's beauty to go underground, beneath their radar, under their consciousness, to reappear as something even smaller.

Worse yet, if parents actually punish their young people when their children love what to them is truly beautiful, the parents will force their youth to lie to everyone, including themselves, and wind their way toward destruction, which will follow either in the form of physical abuse or self-destruction or be exported later on as angry, ruthless business practices on the world. To punish or trivialize the youth for having subtlety of vision is what makes depression an epidemic in modern culture. It is unbelievable that the human heart can survive any of this, but miraculously it does.

When locked away for loving just such an "unknown" boy, a low thing, which Tall Girl's mother has already verbally massacred, the girl's longing for what she loves is transformed into her family weaving obligation which creates a cape of invisibility.

All of us in our youth want to be part of the churning, leaf-popping, spinning, wild, windy, crazy, unknown possibility-filled immensity of the world. This can be done easily and quite beautifully if we have elders who are true individuals, and not just cultural drones, to show us around a bit. Without these mentors and extracurricular visionaries, our children end up lost in their own longing and merge into the immensity with no stable veteran position from which to see it all.

When prohibited from loving the particular and small representations of the immensity of the world, the longing our young people have for the small begins to plot the invisibility of the teenager.

As many of us have, the youth begin to melt into the multiple things of the world, adopting and attaching themselves to anyone and everything that is out there, with no particular form of their own.

Our own faces exist somewhere amongst the natural everyday foment of ordinary things, but if we as youth are not taught to listen to these small things of the world and are forbidden as well to love what we are not, then we are not loved for our particular natures either, whether they are ordinary or extraordinary; we adopt the look, style and thought of whatever captures us first and our real face is never found. We might then become amorphous, unsure of who we are, if it was not for the fact that we have what we love hidden snug behind that invisibility.

For if this thing we love can be understood to be our own beauty, creativity, a seed heart of unsprouted possibility toward which we are pulled by the overwhelming passion of our natural desires, then it is *this* that we hide from our oppressors that can cause us to find our own face in one particular part of the creation.

Our parents and the world that loves us want us as teenagers to stay in the phase of eternal possibility, unsprouted, with a billion choices before us, forever. Although it is true to some degree that, like the Tall Girl, in the hopeful potentiality of our youth we could do anything we want anywhere we please, we cannot ever do it all well. Until we are cut to pieces by life trying to follow the *one* thing we love, we will never leave the world of touching a little of every-thing, instead of being one of those particular things in the immense whole that is worth touching.

No matter how thick the walls of our upbringing or how deeply we are sequestered by what would have us remain general and serv-ing the status quo, if we love well, longing for what we can't see, that which we love finds a way to be with us. It is only a matter of recognizing and accepting the form in which it comes.

We must dig toward the sound of what we love, cut a peephole, make a channel in the walls of our parents' house, a small hole through the restrictive thinking we've grown up with, using the tool of our assigned duties, our creativity adapted to our passion, thereby making an opening so that we can see out of the cocoon-like mores of our upbringing. When we love, we must be creative and make our deceptions beautiful in our forays to get close to the beloved. That is partly how we become artists and true adults.

When we first meet what we love, we could become poets for our longing. When we are removed from what we love, we become singers of grief and weavers of elegant deception. Appearing to mutate and become smaller in form to survive the hardship of absence, as when the Short Boy becomes a hummingbird, actually says that the beloved is gradually forced into its true, original nature, a nature we do not at first always recognize. But even in this tiny original form, what we love about it is not changed and is soon remembered. If the Tall Girl couldn't accept, recognize and love with equal heart the changed form of the little man as an animal, then she would still be stuck as a Tall Girl inside the limited space of her family's need to keep her young, instead of becoming small inside the enormous outer world where she would find her own smaller, unique life. She would be acting like her mother did toward her by not accepting the changed form of what she loves.

And if this tiny transformed thing we love convinces us to leave everything we know, and we go without an elder from outside the family to help us negotiate the world, our desires and our parents, then another danger lurks.

That tiny, shiny thing we love and choose to follow is the child of an immensity, which if we fall into, we could be forever merged and lost as any particular thing either tall or short. Older people of substance and finesse outside the family must help the youth navigate their lives by supporting the youth's inevitable, strange and gorgeous attempt at adulthood while teaching them to dance the edge instead of being swallowed by it into an anonymous state of eternal drifting caused by merging into an ocean of unfocused desire.

No matter what, if we finally follow that shiny little thing we love to the shores of infinite possibility, a jealous wind does blow. Following our heart's desire away from everything we know takes us directly through the merciless winds of the world's jealousy. Anything that loves must be tested by envy. This envious wind who can't stand to see us happy in love or heading toward the ecstasy of our heart's desire would have us poisoned with itself, causing us to lose our love, and make us into life-killing, jealous beings as well.

The story says that the only way we survive the overpowering slyness and unrelenting hatred of the jealousy of the world is for us to be broken down into small, common pieces and reassembled as one small, solid thing by the shiny thing we were following with our heart's desire.

The resentment of those who did not follow their love to a dismembered state will always try to recruit intact young women and men in love with life into the ranks of the cynical armies of jealousy and envy.

Not having to deal with this sort of negativity, as appealing as it may sound, will not bring the young to their own faces or any of us to a useful adulthood.

We become adults only through our losses, not through slick, unblemishing gains. Happiness is not the result but the reward for gestating into a never-before-seen thing that by its small participation in the whole, feeds the world the beauty of our unique remaining form, particular song, walk, plumage and still hopeful eyes.

Sometimes when they hear this tale, people believe the Hummingbird Boy's promise that his beloved's life will be safe as soon as they touch the ocean. This is a Mayan joke. There is no safety, ever. Once you've chosen to love, to have longing, to follow an art or devotion, you automatically accept your death as payment for being blessed with a mortal life to live out your longing.

The difference between diving into an ocean of infinite possibility or dying blown to bits by a jealous wind on the beach of desire rests in the fact that once in that ocean, we trade one kind of numb, trance-like, eternal state of youth for another, exchanging being a child in our parents, little pool for a homogenized life of art pursued but never realized or fulfilled. In the ocean of every possibility, we follow our heart's desire but never make anything distinct or particular. We begin to do everything and what everybody else does, maybe better or worse, but never our own.

To really make beauty, art, or to live artfully one must do it from a particular place, something focused that we get good at no matter how small. Gone is the infinite flowering branch of youth's open-ended possibilities. One flower is chosen, fertilized and hopefully goes to fruit, dries and its seeds go to grow a new flowering beyond the individual. We no longer chase what we desire, we marry what we follow, and cultivate, hatch, raise up what we love.

After the stunning explosion on the shores of possibility, the only thing left standing is what we love. If it is our art we followed here, then like the Hummingbird Boy, it is our art that must put us back together. If it is our love of another person, then it is our love, not that person, which is left standing when that person leaves, that must reassemble us back to life. If it was our love for a dream of peace that we followed to being blown-to-bits on the beach of Days, then it is the power of that shining dream that must put us back together again.

Whether a dream, an art, or love of a person, that shiny little thing we followed is matured through its losses, taught by the natural and unavoidable jealousy of the human existence.

This grief-matured love of ours that was left standing when we that have followed have been dismembered, is what alchemically converts the artist into a magician, the physicist into a devotee of the Divine, a healer into an organic farmer, a shoe salesman into a shoemaker, a queen into a shepherd, a tax collector into a social worker, turning us from the person we have been trained to be, to the person we want to be, and then finally away from either of those into the person we end up becoming.

Art is no longer what we *want* to do, we now do our art to bring the world back to life. The more the scientist investigates, the greater the evidence of the overriding complexity and elegance of what makes the universe happen. Healers decide to farm to make the bodies healthy, instead of always fixing what is broke. It is no longer enough to rebel, resist or make a revolution, we must live out the story in all its aspects, realizing that the hero of that story is not the girl, the hummingbird, ourselves or what we love. The hero of this story is the story itself.

So often the artist is sacrificed for the art and the art is what lives. This story tells us that our art must be sacrificed, turned into a magic that puts us back together in a new way and hatches the world back to life. The story tells us that living the life of an artist is not as useful as living our lives as a work of art.

What we love and what brought us into the world must together hatch us back into life, but this time not into what we were but into a never-before-seen thing, all its own, whose voice cries in ecstasy, whose form goes even beyond our own imaginings.

The hardest part of being a parent is to sit like a mother bird on our children's egg of possibilities without meddling or peeking or having any say as the young person is allowed to go through all the painful, mysterious, unexplained and even toxic changes necessary for them to arrive at their true form.

Though at some point your daughter's desire may drive her, like the Tall Girl speaking beautiful words to her short, unseen lover, to read the poems of thirteenth century, ecstatic Persians out loud to the lonely walls of her bedroom in secret hopes that some lover would mistake her for God and come in through the eaves, it could be that somewhat later when the harshness of the jealous world has taken her tenderness apart, it will be her art, her poetry, her desire to be seen as someone who "sees" that will reassemble her into a real person with a grief-tempered joy in one eye and a fierce compassion in the other.

Like it or not, a million moltings occur in a fully lived life, and the story says that all the fights, conniving, fleeing, crying, dying, grief and confusion are the entangled roots on the tree of life upon whose branches our adulthood must come to fruition. It says if we haven't left home, tried hard and failed, fallen apart and allowed ourselves to be re-membered back to life in our mother's cooking pot by the small, unpopular shiny never-before-seen thing you believed in, then you are not yet human.

The story doesn't say our fathers will improve or that our mothers will lose their need to control or meddle, but it does say the father continues to keep his world alive by carrying the Sun and the mother keeps her world in order and the daughter and the hummingbird's ecstatic love-making brings the rain to moisten the patient earth's thirsty heart.

Second Layer: In a Net of Stars

The Indigenous Understanding

Like a clever flock of ragged crones from some old Irish tale who rear an orphaned prince as a baby in the wilds, hiding his true status in the garb and speech of regular folk in hopes of keeping him well and the world ignorant of his royalty until his own strength and wisdom can grow into a size fair enough to cope on equal ground with those assassins of his parents who would eliminate, enslave or trivialize him to keep him from the throne, the Tzutujil Maya as well keep alive their more subtle and sacred understandings by hiding them like royal children in a coded language deep inside the common trappings of certain well-known stories like *The Daughter of the Sun.*

In this ingenious way most every aspect of what is holy to indigenous people can be kept alive, unsuspected inside a story, though told over and over, remaining disguised inside an ancient sacred metaphor undisturbed by the casual listener who only hears an equally useful inspiring tale about the individual struggles of someone like themselves.

However, after hearing the story many times, as serious listeners we tend to end up riding the heartbreak and beauty of our original understanding of the tale like we would a flying horse who instinctively leaps into the next layer where a more sacred meaning lies hidden like an exiled prince in the wilder nature of the reader's own spiritual landscape. If this goes on long enough, one day our comprehension of the tale is strong enough to wrestle with the spirit-killing jealousy of our own rationalist minds whose initial lack of metaphor ability might want to destroy or trivialize the royalness of our own natural sense of mystery and organic imaginations. The distance we must go insures that the secret the story holds remains safe from greedy, impatient minds who treat knowledge as a mined or captured possession instead of a gradual living thing we must maintain and cultivate in the ground.

Our love for that incredible thing we find there, through our deeper listening, changes us from naïve pups suckling on the story's milk into cultural parents who long to hold and feed the story itself, just like we would the orphaned cub of an endangered animal, a precious child or our own Indigenous Souls. Only then does the spirit who hides in the story feel sufficiently respected to reveal its true identity.

The understandings in this second layer of *The Daughter of the Sun* are those of initiated Tzutujil to whom the story belongs. It is the remembering of what the spirits are doing during an annual cycle that occurs in nature upon which all human life is dependent but whose telling is disguised seamlessly inside an ornate and brilliant metaphor as a story about human relationships.

Like people everywhere, human relationships are of great interest to the Tzutujil people. However, to the initiated individual, a story ceases to fascinate unless in its telling the normal ruminations of village gossip, family failures, love affairs and the struggle of the individual are incorporated into the story as a way to describe the hidden story of nonhuman spirits whose daily life we see as rocks, plants, animals, sky, earth and weather, whose annual cycles are the family histories of what the Mayan know to be the Divine.

The graciousness of this ancient way of learning through stories such as *The Daughter of the Sun* comes not only from our being allowed to identify with one or more of the characters and the lives they live out in the story, but from the realization of what Mayans have had to relearn in every generation; that though we as listeners have the illusion that we have jumped into the story, the story has actually jumped into us and uses our lives to tell out its story.

To the Tzutujil the everyday lives through which we struggle are Holy because the sacred use our lives to live out their own stories. Every instance of human folly, beauty, naiveté, our hatreds, pettiness, jealousy, overreactions, betrayals, and omissions and seemingly meaningless events become vessels for the Divine to show themselves. For a traditional Tzutujil, not every addiction and neurosis needs to be straightened out, fixed or transcended, for most of what makes us suffer are inevitabilities with which we have no choice but to contend and which, try as we might, cannot always be sidestepped because the Spirit of the Big Story keeps them in our lives for the story to continue.

Our lives, then, no matter how chaotic, uneventful, failure-filled, suffering, safe or dangerous we perceive them to be, become a canoe into which the Divine steps to row us with paddles made of story away from the shores of oblivion and spiritual amnesia, over the terrifying seas of chance and wonder to camp on the shores of little islands of possibility.

In this story-method of learning, we humans become part of the geography of nature, important not because of our inventories of conquests, or chronicles of having been victimized, or our labor-saving inventions that kill this geography, or our egalitarianism or our capacity to get to heaven, but just for having been born and showing up for work, the work of living out our part of the story.

The Daughter of the Sun lives out its life in the striking land-scape of the Tzutujil Maya in the central part of the southwestern region of Guatemala, in the area of the Old Tzutujil Kingdom as it was before Europeans crashed in on them in 1524. These Mayan people, though once spread out, were gathered by the invaders, into a conglomerate village of mixed clans and Tzutujil subgroups renamed and marked on maps as Santiago Atitlan. Known as *Chichoyá* by most other Mayan highlanders, and as *Ch jay* by the people who live there, this town is situated on a point of fertile vol-canic dust that bulges from the shoreline of what might be the most mesmerizing lake of the entire world.

The Tzutujil villagers call this deep lake *C'tie Ya* or Mother Waters. The lake whose formal ceremonial name is *Rumuxux Ruchiuleu* or Belly Button of the Earth is a steep, gargantuan vol-canic caldron filled with a shifting water whose colors range from iris purples to turquoise stone to liquid jade green. Sitting on the edge of this caldron and forming a fence that seems to burst straight out of the lake are three very tall more or less inactive volcanic cones which are heavily forested and wrinkled with hundreds of canyons and ridges.

Though each is named in Mayan for the subjects of various sacred stories, the middle one that looms to the southeast of the village and lake is known as Our Grandmother volcano. It is here at the top that the Sun Father in the story joins the Grandmother Moon during their lunchtime rendezvous.

Even farther south between the volcanic mountain stronghold of the Tzutujil and the coastal plains that hug the ocean, a crinkly labyrinth of mist-covered river canyons and convoluted hills fan out like an alligator's gnarled front foot. The young lovers' failed flight to safety toward the kingdom of the Ocean took them over this verdant barricade of rugged cliffs into a narrow canyon down a rough river chasm which they followed to the beach.

The Hummingbird and the Horned Guan made their home in these mysterious cloud forest canyons and live there still. This magical impenetrable zone between the mountains and the coastal ocean is considered to be the Female Earth by the Tzutujil of today, and is still called *Izoc Juyu, Izoc Taqaaj,* meaning "Woman Hill, Woman Valley."

Between these wild hills and the ocean brims a coastal savanna dotted with grand and gracious trees. Some of them flower in fuchsia or solid yellow, while others are so big, continuously growing and ancient that in parts of the coast, entire tribal populations could meet and live, trade or make their ceremonies beneath them. Though once a powerful, steaming rain forest, these individual survivors of those days hold their stories privately as they stretch their majesties over the cleared cane, cattle and cotton land whose grassy lowland plain slides straight to the great thundering Pacific Ocean who pummels and grinds the sparkling black sand beaches.

Though living just sixty miles away and called affectionately "Grandmother Waters" or "The Old Eyebrows of Sea Foam," the ocean has been seen by only one in five hundred Tzutujil villagers. Those people who'd actually dared to bathe in the ocean were looked upon like the first astronauts just returned from the moon and were the source of constant wonder.

This strip of land then, some 30 miles wide in southwest Guatemala that runs from the cool Lake Atitlan down those sixty miles through rough hills and muggy coastal plains to the hot black sand of the churning Grandmother Ocean is what the Tzutujil know to be the spiritual body of their people whose heart, or Placental Soul, must be ritually fed and spiritually sustained by the tribe for whom the landscape is a suckling parent in the most literal sense. To the Tzutujil traditionalist the land is not some kind of detached matter that has a soul, but is a tangible living soul that has a heart. This soul of the tribal Earth feeds the people with what the wild and cultivated lands produce, which is known as the face of the Divine; and the people in turn are required to feed and maintain its heart. One of the sustaining foods of that heart is the telling of the story of *The Daughter of the Sun* and the rituals for which it forms a map of remembrance.

One of the traditional understandings in the tale is that the great, endless ocean contains an unseen and unknown world whose boundaries are infinite. The child of this immense possibility is he who comes to court the Daughter of the Sky Gods, the Sun and the Moon, who think that all they can see from their tall mountains is all there is and all that's worth seeing. Like literalists everywhere, they refuse to look beyond what they cannot measure or possess deeming it too "small" to count. They also refuse to look deep inside anything, deeming that too "particular" for their immense general way of seeing.

With great humor, all Mayans recognize themselves in the story when they hear how the arrogant Sun and temperamental Moon consider this narrow body of land to be a finite kingdom, over which they rule as the only possible world, choosing to forget the vast inner kingdom of the ocean out of which even Mayans feel all life had its origins.

This is a commentary on the inevitable human problem of tribalism and the tragic results of ethnocentricity. It reminds us that a preoccupation with purity is a sign that a people have lost their real stories, lost their place in history, lost their land and relationship with nature and in an effort to be "someone" they engineer mythologies that are rationalist inventions to corroborate a pure ancestry. This same rationalism probably killed their stories and Indigenous relationship with the land to begin with. The story of their cultural loss should be their story, and from that grief they could grow a new culture. If you go back far enough, all people are mixed no matter what they say, and that is no disgrace.

The story also says that a peoples' deep attachment to their homeland and customs is necessary, wonderful and life-giving, but should never be allowed to fuel a destructive chauvinism that excludes the rest of the world's love for its own life and land.

The alternate forms by which the Tzutujil Divine Beings disguise themselves in this amazing narrative run from the most common, transparent, sacred puns to a polyvalent ornateness that takes years to comprehend.

The most obvious of the easy ones, of course, are the Sun and the Moon.

When they bring to life *The Daughter of the Sun,* Mayan storytellers never actually call the Tall Girl's parents the Sun or the Moon.

The father they call *Cdta,* which literally means "Our Father." Likewise when referring to Tall Girl's mother she is named *C tit* and this of course translates as "Our Grandmother."

These are the very terms with which all villagers directly address the Sun and Moon when they pray and the names they use for them when speaking about them to another Tzutujil. The direct words for the Sun and the Moon, *Q ij* and *Ic ,* respectively, are used sparingly and only when both orbs are absent from the sky; for they are terms used to talk about them as objective phenomena instead of speaking to them as blood relatives.

"Our Father" and "Our Grandmother" are never far from us and are a comfort to any villager no matter how far from home he may have drifted, but to address them as the Sun or the Moon would be to invite alienation and an unthinkable breach of Mayan etiquette, tantamount to someone addressing their Irish grandmother to her face with, "Hey you, old Celtic female Homo Sapiens."

Until Tall Girl mysteriously appears with a short, shiny sweetheart, the life her family and the Village of the Gods leads would be familiar to any Tzutujil villager.

The Mayans, however, do not consider the story to have been modeled after their daily human lives, but rather the lives and annual routines to which villagers are subjects are patterned and set down by the way the Deities go about their lives in their "other," parallel worlds. To the people the stories are how we learn to do everyday things from the Gods. The story shows us not only what the Gods did in the beginning but what they continue to do today and how the things we do in our daily lives are part of what the Gods are doing right now. The result of the Gods' normal village routines looks to us in this world as natural phenomena: from where we stand sweating in our fields, the Father Sun looks to us like something perfectly round and incredibly hot that hangs above, traveling the sky. But in the Sun's world the sky is firm ground, a mountain where he works too hard, gets overheated and trudges home hungry, exhausted and grumpy, eats, goes to sleep and goes back at dawn to work. Uninitiated people only see the sun coming up, climbing the sky, sinking into the night earth and hopefully rising anew upon the following day.

Whereas, those that know the story and understand it, try to feed the Sun to help him in his struggles, participating instead of staring at him like a faraway thing. Sacred beings do not live in a world isolated and distant from our own in states of repose or as chess game manipulators of a separate world of matter. The Gods work, suffer, sing, weep, get sad, become ecstatic, have children and die, albeit their deaths are always some kind of transformation.

The rocks work, the winds work, the rivers work, the animals all work, the weather works, everything works, and in the story these deities work like us, but in our daily lives rocks don't appear as admirers and handsome suitors of the Daughter of the Moon who hold up the sky unless we've heard the story and therefore understand that as we climb over them, the seemingly slow life of rocks has a secret life that they are living out in another dimension right alongside of our own.

The Deities are not the Gods of the trees, or the sun or the fire, the moon, or the ocean; they *are* the Trees, the Sun, the Fire, the Moon and the Ocean, etc. They stand before us tangible and inter-related, but also live their lives as Deities in the other world, whose lives are being spoken into life by the other layers of Deities who tell the story we all live out.

The Tzutujil people try to help the Sun walk the sky and assist the Moon to keep her house of the Earth by doing their everyday human work well in their human layer of life, work whose intricacies and style they inherited from their hard-working Gods.

Like the Sun, every day, Tzutujil men of all ages rise before dawn, carrying their heavy tools over their shoulders as much as twenty miles to their fields or the forest where they struggle without modern machinery of any kind and against all probability to miraculously coax food, fiber and fuel from the volcanic ash of the volcano slopes. And like the Sun, they return loaded with up to 100 pounds of care-fully split firewood, avocados, edible greens, corn or the like, bar-reling through the compound threshold exhausted, "sun" burnt, single-focused, hungry and edgy. Though admired for their heroic struggle, some men, like the Sun, are so thoroughly overworked and underfed that they can hardly participate in the family, having to sleep early enough to rise again before dawn. Not a few men have succumbed and died before their time.

Tzutujil mothers quite out loud and directly call themselves the

Ral Ctit, Daughter of the Moon, and because everyone is born from a mother, we call the Moon "Our Grandmother." The women like to see themselves hard at work doing what that beautiful Tall Girl did in her life.

Women work just as hard as men, and if the men die, the women work even harder. After hauling water on their heads from the lake to their huts, grinding corn, chasing children around, washing the clothes in the lake, tending their fowl, hoeing their gardens, making deals in the market, they lean back into their backstrap looms where they weave all the family's clothing in the style that the Daughter of the Sun and Moon invented and continues to do in the other world. Every traditional lady will tell her daughters from an early age onward that the reason women do what they do and the way they do it in that style is because the Moon taught them to do it in that manner. They feel in some direct way that each of them is the single daughter of the Moon and that they are all helping her to live by doing their life according to the specifications of her excellence.

If they have grown children, old enough to responsibly watch over the younger ones, or if all the children are grown, many Tzutujil women, just like the Moon, arrange to meet their husbands at midday for lunch out in the hills. Willing to walk the many steep and rocky miles, they arrive at the fields loaded up with pots of stews and drinkable things, handmade corn cakes or tortillas. It is usually a long way off to bring a man his lunch, which he could have probably brought along, but the custom is never questioned because behind it lies another secret.

The extended family compounds are filled with one room, single-family huts. To have intimate times alone with your wife or husband in the relentless commotion of the family hub is impossible to begin with; on top of that, because they are the greatest blessings of their lives together, it would never occur to the parents to ask their children to leave them in peace. Once you have children, that one room, no matter how rich or poor, spacious or tiny, becomes their room, and there is no time or place for sweethearts to be alone together.

That's why, like the Sun and the Moon, men and women meet out in the woods, "eating their lunch together," which is a code for making love far away from the *rchi il,* or the hubbub of the village. And like the Sun and Moon, their children are often conceived in the fields, in the mountains, which is felt to fertilize and further bless the ground while giving the family sustenance as well. The world is fertilized by the love-making of Sun and Moon at noon, and Tall Girl was probably made out in the sky hills beneath the chocolate bean tree of the summit. Though it is a known fact that men and women who love each other have the best cornfields and harvest yields, the secret of their noontime meetings is not something people yell about in public. It is kept sacred and quiet for the sanity of married people.

This secrecy has caused problems, off and on, with outsiders. Not a few zealous Peace Corp volunteers, social workers and feminist advocates from big cities or nonvillage cultures have been stoned, avoided or gossiped out of the village by the Tzutujil women themselves after the activists tried to stop the women from participating in what the outsiders saw as a "deplorable custom offensive to women, who are forced to carry loads long distances to men too lazy to pack them."

There were even sheltered children in the town who hadn't pieced together the motive behind their mother's solitary visits to the hills any more than Tall Girl suspected that the Moon's visit to the sky was nothing more than her feeding the Sun.

The poor girl is not even allowed to have a boyfriend, fall in love, much less marry or make love. When a mysterious shimmering short boy whose origins are unknown all of the sudden emerges as the girl's clandestine sweetheart, they don't wander secretly off somewhere, they don't even touch. Instead, they praise each other in the ancient initiation language akin to a village shaman's praying.

Like little kids coming in from the cold when they smell the aroma of food, we listeners who are inside the story up until then can now watch the story jump into us as it begins to cook something wild and brilliant.

When the Tall Girl is scolded, beaten, misunderstood, punished and isolated, the listeners want to exterminate the Moon and think that the mysterious identity of the Shortboy is solved when he enters the dark cloister of his sweetheart as the never-before-seen Hummingbird. But what does it mean that he turns out to be the son of the powerful Grandmother Ocean and the Hurricane? What? This tiny bird is their son? How could it be?

He is the "sparkle of the Ocean" turned into a small flying warrior bird. The Ocean flashing of the Hummingbird is secretly known as the sparkle of the ocean's water off the flashing of the fins of certain whales. Hummingbird's father is a Hurricane, and Hurricane's animal soul is the whale or what is known as the lightning fish, *Caypa' Ch ú* .

The word *hurricane* is originally a Mayan word, *huraqan,* meaning "one footed," or the whale. The term was hauled to Europe, flayed off its story by returning Spaniards and entered the English language devoid of any care for its rich birth, a lot like Hummingbird Boy.

But the flash off the Ocean and the Whale is their son, and in other tales this flash is known to be the first human being.

Tall Girl, however, at their meeting, like most of us when in love, cares not one gopher louse whether her lover is from here or there; her heart just loves him.

If the Short Boy ends up being the "flashing of the salty Ocean," then who is this deep pool, deer-eyed, water-pot carrying, beautiful Tall Girl?

She is fresh water.

The story of *The Daughter of the Sun* is the life and struggle of fresh water as the daughter of the powerful, rigid Sun and the temperamental, changeable Moon.

While to some this may not seem so grand a secret, to the Tzutujil and most of the people of the world, water is the holiest and most crucial life-giving element in the Universe. That water is the child of the fiery Sun and the niece of other hot stars is scientifically well known, but the depths and ramifications of these connections are only just beginning to surface through the work of astronomers, astrophysicists, and scientists of many disciplines. Some say that the Sun is fusing hydrogen. When you burn hydrogen in this atmosphere, you get water. Water is indeed the Daughter of the Sun.

During my time with Tzutujil shaman Nicolas Chiviliu, I was taught over and over how water is the physical manifestation of the Divine Female in the Universe. When Tzutujil women identify with the Tall Girl, considering themselves at the very least her direct descendants, they are identifying with all the fresh water in the world. Like Tall Girl, as little girls they are springs or water hidden in plants like the jungle dahlia, who secretes water in its stalk during the dry season. As grown women, their patroness is *C'tie Ya,* "Our Mother Waters," the lake on which they live. Old women come to be the great salt womb of Grandmother Ocean. Every baby girl, young woman, child-bearing mother, matron and crone, no matter how many names they go through in a lifetime, all have the syllable *Ya* before their names. *Ya* means water. In the village, women are water.

The story is the saga of how the original nature of the cycles of water as the collective soul of the Tribal geography, the Earth Body of the Mayan world, came about. The suffering and beautiful fate of water has been the same ever after, repeating itself every year. This is her story.

Though often translated as "heart," the word *Rukux* actually refers to the center of a placenta, meaning the forming child. In the Tzutujil language of the original story, the *Rukux* of corn seed, for instance, is that magical part of the kernel that causes it to sprout, or alternately the *Rukux* is that part of the corn kernel that causes it, in its death by having been eaten, to put flesh on the consumer's bones. The soul to the Mayans is not as intangible as it is in other parts of the world.

This might be because the *Rukux,* "heart or soul" of something, for everything has one, is what contains water. The soul is the water, and the Earth is the Placental Heart-container for the water, and what water does is life itself.

This is why in Mayan the *Rukux* also refers to the placenta as well as the expectant mother's heart. It is the liquid that both contain that gives life.

The people say that upon conceiving a child, a mother's beating heart divides itself into two sacks of liquid: one for her that grows back to normal size in her chest and one for her child who grows up inside, developing its own *Rukux.* The human and animal heart is a rhythmic placenta through which our "water" keeps singing life into us.

When we finally see that she is water, Tall Girl is suddenly recognized to be the living *Rukux,* or Placental Heart of the Flowering Earth, the same Earth that suckles us as a mother and upon whom we as spiritual amnesiacs are still accepted as one of her flowering bushes.

Like the human mother who divides her heart to make her children, the Tall Girl who is the Earth's water-filled heart is doing the same thing when she is divided by the cruel lightning blast of her jealous uncle. Her heart becomes the diverse *Rukux* of all life forms, leaving enough of her own heart to grow her own smaller particular form with a life small enough with which to love another small particular being. An intact Goddess is too big for any small being to love alone.

Though all of this is what adult villagers know this tale to hold, the deeper, more terrifying understanding into which the story conspires to immerse our forgetful hearts is the complacent harshness of how every being in the story is determined to posses the Water for themselves.

It doesn't take much to see that in the human realm. People and Gods only want to "own" the female principle of life, they don't want to love her.

Just like the Gods and every being on that story's earth, we mistake her dedicated, life-giving presence in our veins, in the leave's stems, in the atmosphere as clouds, in aquifers and animals as the water in the House of the Moon, as the Earth itself, thinking her holy presence to be an unquestioned right, oblivious to the fact that water is a generous visitation from the Holy Female without whom all life would cease. She is the greatest possible gift and could easily take herself away.

Once we learn this, we must hear the story again, read it again, have it read to us again. Then we see the life-cycle of the water that we thought we knew so well and wonder why the Sun and Moon's beautiful Water Daughter is called Tall Girl?

When the Grandmother Moon discovered that short, shiny boy courting her tall, diligent daughter, the old woman felt the water of her own youth begin to leak out of her control toward the Ancient Ocean.

The Ocean's child is forced to concentrate his brilliant ocean sparkle into a small bird in order to bring his shine to where his beloved Fresh Water girl has been dammed up inside the House of the Moon. The Moon's House is, of course, the mountain stronghold of the central Guatemalan highlands. When the Grandmother tries to restrict, isolate and dam up her watery daughter, she is still trying to keep her as the other half of her heart and not willing to recognize that the daughter is grown too big to contain. The damming signifies the annual springtime massing of fresh waters held in the overflowing springs and rock pools of the mountains, called *C wa ya* , and known ironically in Spanish as *presas,* or prisons.

When this fresh mountain water falls in love, she ends up fleeing down and away from the mountains to escape the stone prison of the Moon, drawn by the sparkle of the Ocean straight to the salty sea.

In other words the short, flat, salt water of the infinite broad Ocean has successfully courted and convinced the tall, fresh water of the high mountains to overflow the stone walls of the springs and fill up the dry river beds and rush as a flooding springtime river down the hills, through the plains, straight to the sea.

The beautiful water daughter is called *Ya Nim Ruqan Xtan* or Tall Girl because in this part of Water's life she becomes a long river course connecting the Sky God's high mountains with the flat rippling Ocean.

It is obvious then why her sweetheart is known as the Short Boy, because he is from the lowlands and the ocean, which hasn't any "height" but does have an undetermined depth. The Sky Gods of the mountains cannot recognize him or any value in him because they only value tallness and have difficulty appreciating deepness.

Because these Gods are beings of heat and height, the Sun doesn't really know much about his Daughter either, for as a wet being, a water being, her depth is not fathomed or even recognized by him.

Because the world becomes green again in the spring from the freshness of his daughter's female water, Tall Girl is said to be weaving the World into flower, keeping the Sun adorned and his world alive. For this he wants to keep all the fresh water in his domain.

It is the Sun's nature not to know that his own heat and bright light causes his daughter's water to flow and evaporate, and it is his grand reflection that causes the Hummingbird to shine, all of which draws the daughter toward the Ocean.

In the beginning there was only one season in the mountains and another season on the sea. This story of *The Daughter of the Sun* tells how the annual cycle of seasons came about to be one half of the year dry, hot and windy and the other half wet and rainy.

At first the Sun held total sovereignty over the solid earth and would have melted the rocks and burned up the world if the Moon and her liquid daughter had not poured their water over his over-heated head to make the rainless clouds of the dry season.

All Mayan people say the Moon is the keeper of the water, especially in the dry seasons, when her daughter is under her supervision and control, staying at home weaving the beings of the world into their water-filled and flowering forms.

While the Sun keeps time, regular time, daily time, and yearly time, the Moon is in charge of regulating moments and cycles, controlling the birth, growth and death of plants and animals through the pulses of her daughter's water.

When her daughter begins to have natural impulses of her own instead of pulses controlled by the Moon, the old lady loses control. The Moon's hysterical arrogance over her daughter's love for a "short" boy of unknown origins is actually a code that translates: the Moon doesn't want her own personal, perfect, virgin water to be lost into the all-consuming Ocean where her daughter will merge into a female bigger than herself, becoming common and accessible to all.

When the Water is kept imprisoned in the rock house of the Moon, the daughter's weepings are sometimes called the first rain of spring, and the thumping of her magical loom is the first faraway thunder.

But these tears are salty like the Ocean, and when they drop upon the girl's enforced weaving, they make a cloth of invisibility.

When the boy and girl don these capes in their desperate and dangerous elopement, it signifies, among others things, that the world is covered in such a dense cape of leaves and flowers and the riverbank so overgrown from her water daughter's imprisonment that from the haughty altitude of the Moon and Sun the ocean-bound river course filled with their daughter's substance cannot be seen beneath the lush forest canopy. The riotous exuberance of the Earth's annual rebirth of plants, budding trees and flowers is the grief of Water, but the overwhelming density and spell of its aroma intoxicates us to a point of amnesia. The origination of this gift is obscured by the immensity of the gift and remains invisible to a world drunk on its beauty.

The jealousy that the North Wind bears both the girl and the boy throughout comes from the fact that they pose a threat to the dry season. As Lord over all dryness, the fact that the boy is ocean water courting fresh water makes him hate the couple to begin with. But if they ever marry, they will have rain clouds for children, and these clouds no doubt will rise up from the Ocean as they do today at the beginning of the wet season on return visits to their grandparents, the Sun and the Moon, bringing their youthful rainstorms along.

The Water Daughter's run to the Ocean as a Long River and the resultant rainstorms that return to rain on the highlands signify the end of the dry season. This would put Q iq out of business, as it does now for six months.

Because he is grumpy and dry and hates the water, he won't have any watery females bossing his dryness around. Q iq will never let the girl reach the Ocean and hates his brother the Sun for loving water as his daughter.

Originally Lightning and Rain didn't go together. Lightning came from the sky and Rain from beneath the Ocean. On account of what happens in the story Lightning, Rain, Fog, Mist, Clouds, Hail, certain winds, Floods and Rains have all combined forces, for they are now blood relatives, ever since the Sky and Ocean became in-laws through the marriage of the Hummingbird to the Tall Girl.

Ironically, when Q iq the dry North Wind shoots and dismembers his water niece with stolen lightning, he is unwittingly performing a sacrifice for rain, a sacrificial ritual which was until very recently understood among all Maya in one form or another, but one that is relatively common in scattered areas.

Lightning is thought to come from stone, and from stone, all fire. For this reason all the sky Gods in the story are fire brothers, volcanic mountain sons of stone.

Strike two flints together in the dark and see the sparks jump, the stone light up; and smell the ozone. To the Tzutujil all arrowheads, glass knives, obsidian microflakes not only contain the fire of lightning but are the tools of lightning. All the Sun's brothers are the various types of lightning, those ancient beings who taught humans how to make knifelike tools. When villagers find ancient implements chipped from stone, they know them to be the tips of lightning weapons and are revered as such.

The wind dismembering the fresh water by means of a stone knife i.e., lightning, is a code for two further serious understandings.

First, that in the spring, fierce winds arise that evaporate the earth's water over the stones in the heat of the Sun such as to dissipate all water and make the Earth dryer than it already is, but this same water-dismembering wind raises the water from the ground into the sky as clouds.

The other knowledge hidden here is how at the end of every dry season, a sparkling oscellated turkey is to be sacrificed to bring the rain. The beautiful bird is named for the Water Girl herself, who we hope will return. The animal, after much ceremony, praying, cajoling and many explanations, is killed and cut into many particular pieces, each of which represents a part of the entire world in microcosm, killed and dismembered by a stone knife, or one that is called lightning knife or lightning spike. The head is given to this part of the land, the heart to another, the legs to other another, parts of the chest, the wings and so on, all to feed different districts of the water-starved earth. The remainder of the meat is cooked and eaten by the people. Called *ptix,* the pot used to cook the sacrificial bird is exactly of the same type as in the story demanded of the Moon by the bereaved Hummingbird.

It is easy to see how the North Wind's horrid misogynist hatred of the Holy Female Water and the fact that as wind he can't possess her are partly behind why he kills her.

As humans, we see that there are men who do this to women, and that is unimaginably wrong. On a Mayan side of that, we see humans today, both men and women, endorsing or doing the same thing to the Female Water and natural Earth, and that is a crime of equal stature.

Why do we feel the same responsibility and loss that every sacred being in the tale feels when Tall Girl is blown to pieces? Because we are as guilty as the Gods and miss Her just as much. The story wants us to feel this guilt and grief that through them we gain the deepest understanding of the story of how the Water Goddess, the Female principle of the world, instead of dividing her heart in two to make one more child, is herself as the single placental heart of the Earth divided into the myriad forms of all diverse things that make this world what it is. Everything we see, eat, love or condemn in Nature is a piece of her.

Humans know her best in her dismemberment. When she was still an intact young water Goddess in the house of the Moon, in the Village of the Sun, her womb, i.e., the lake, contained the embryonic, unhatched dream forms of every possibility of life. Her explosion into all these beings leaves her husband holding her bodiless heart when they marry.

This is a grown-up understanding, away from the trance of mis-interpreted one-god religions and no-god idealisms, which assumes the world is dead matter and just lets us suckle. The story shakes us awake into the terrifying reality that we humans have only our creativity in ritual and story-language ability as a gift to the Female principle of the universe whose annual dismemberment at our hands and the natural cycles of Nature's Divine gives us our entire life, our food, our homes, all the fiber, water and each other.

In as much as the North Wind shoots the Earth's water, dispersing it with the electric heat from the Heart of the Sky, it is the Hummingbird that is put into motion as well. The winds that rise off the Ocean are known to the Tzutujil as life-giving winds who oppose Q iq , but who cannot conquer him. The Hummingbird as child of the Hurricane is the youngest and gentlest of these sibling winds out of the south and as such are called *Xcamiel.*

When the Hummingbird "blows" back to the highlands with the body of his beloved, dismembered Water Sweetheart on his back, the Tzutujil understand this as a polite ritual code for how the life-giving Southern Wind "flys" back up to the highlands with clouds on his back, causing the real, hard rains of spring, understood as the weeping of the world on his return to the girl's home.

Fresh water therefore returns to her home on the back of the South Wind, dismembered into life-giving clouds, causing the world to weep the first rains of spring. Just as the fresh water rushed, confused and in love, to the Ocean, so gently and gradually the Hummingbird wind travels back up the same wild river course over the same hills and canyons to return the world's soul back to the grief-stricken Earth. In Guatemala we can see this every spring.

The Tzutujil are very clear about how they understand that the results of the eternal and annual battle between the cold, dry sky mountain wind and the warm, mild wet winds of the Ocean causes as its byproduct the cycles of alternating fertility and dryness that make life as they know it a possibility. They say the Southern Winds think that it should be wet all the time and Q iq wants it always dry. Like humans, both opposing sides believe their "tribe" of Gods has all the answers, and the great Mayan understanding says it is the continuance of their self-centered and energetic opposition that keeps life moving in cycles of rebirth and maturation.

Before this gentle, grief-soaked Hummingbird Wind walks that river course back to the Sun's Mountain stronghold, he packs "the clouds," the evaporated water, into various plant leaves. It is easy to understand how this signifies the way trees drink up her water-body and hold it there, cherished, in their leaves. So Water is a Goddess hiding inside plants, thereby making them live. Water has now taken the form of plants. Because water is what allows all plants to be plants, the Hummingbird Wind rolls the cloud water of dismembered ground water into the leaves of all the plants.

Because plants are recognized by the unique shapes and qualities of their leaves, the Hummingbird is essentially calling a complete roll call of all the forms that water takes when she turns into plants. It is exactly this roll call in which village shamans immerse the greater part of their waking hours.

Water has escaped the rocky prisons of the Moon's springs in the Mountain Stronghold of the Sun's sky, and in love with the sparkle of the Ocean, seeps secretly through the Mountains, gathering in hopeful streams, to rush as a long swollen river to the Ocean, where dismembered by the dry electric heat of the sky, she lives on in a massive diversity as all the world's plants, whose tree and plant breaths become the clouds carried on the back of the Southern Hummingbird Wind back to her origination in the mountain lake. Inside the pot (the lake) under the Moon's bed (the night sky) she is then "cooked" like the wild greens that the Mayans love and depend on daily for their food, and it is here that water finally goes from plant form to become all the animals hatched from eggs and born from wombs.

In other words, since all animals either eat vegetation or some other animal that does, they get the water last, and in the story the Mayans are saying that water turns into the animals hatched by the Moon back to life.

In order to bring his beloved's "clouds" and "plant" body back to the village of the Sky Gods, the Hummingbird boy packs her plant wrapped pieces into a netted string bag, called *Yaal*.

To this day, in Guatemala, these net bags are in common use and can be seen many times a day, swollen with heavy loads of wild fruit, edible greens or cultivated harvests, on the backs of Mayan men returning on foot from the coastal hills. Initiated men know and address the heavy, sweet-smelling load under which they daily struggle as, "The Daughter of the Grandmother."

Though these nets are an ancient Mayan tool and the one that the Hummingbird Boy employed was none other than one of these common net bags, they contain a secret that transforms their commonness into a sacred dimension whereby a regular farmer doing his familiar work is knowingly participating in a ritual activity that originates from this story and in doing so, does his part to keep the Divine Female alive.

These net bags are made using a magical measurement determined by the interrelationship of the distances between certain joints of the farmer's body and the amount of land that he can work in one day.

This working man takes very stiff, two-ply maguey fiber cord that he has twined by hand upon his thighs and measures it off thirteen times the distance between the sternum covering his heart and the tip of his middle finger on the hand of the farmer's outstretched left arm.

With this he then determines one side of a square out in the woods within which he can accomplish one day's work of cutting trees, another day clearing brush, another day splitting the wood, another day hauling it home, and then one day turning the earth with a foot plow, another day planting, etc.

When he clears the trees and brush off this square of land determined by the measurement off his chest, he leaves the trees that sit at the corners. Because the world is the Sun's field that he works, whose measurements are taken from his chest, corresponding to Sun-ups and Sun-downs, the trees at the corners of a farmer's field are his personal versions of the Sun's volcanic trunks that hold up the sky at the corners of the world.

As a man works his field, the Sun works his, and both keep time alive by working within the measured Sun-ups of their comings and goings.

With this same distance of cord a net bag is knotted together that can hold as much as that farmer can carry on his back. The Sun has one as well, but in his every knot is a star: the net of stars in the sky. It is in such a netted bag that the Hummingbird, sad and enraged, packed all the parts of the Water Girl he loved.

In the beginning of the story one doesn't see the boy working or sweating, only loving and enchanting. The Sun, on the other hand, only works. When Hummingbird Boy uses a net bag of this type to carry the water back to the mountain, everyone knows that something has happened to him and he is no longer a boy or a teenager, but is now doing what men do. The story now says, what men do is hard and comes from loss.

Though the Hummingbird's transformation into a shaman and a man could have only taken place after he has passed through his losses and become an adult working person, when this Southern Wind, Hummingbird, son of Ocean, loaded down like a workingman, returns to the village from the Female Coastal Earth, like Tzutujil men do today, he is greeted and treated as someone who has struggled to bring home to the village what it needs in order to live.

When as the Southern Wind he arrives carrying the Moon's daughter home in this dismembered state, the Moon wants her daughter back in her original form, with the same face that she drove away with her insistence. But when the Moon says she wants to have her daughter back, she means she wants the world's fresh water that is hiding from her in the diversity of plants to return to the jurisdiction of the Moon, as one water.

The story says the Hummingbird shaman can revive the Water Daughter only if her mother the Moon works along beside him and obeys his every instruction. This is a Tzutujil way of saying that ever since those times, the repentant Moon works in conjunction with the wind and the Ocean, as evidenced by the ebb and flow of the sea tides.

However, the Hummingbird shaman when replying to the Moon uses the famous Tzutujil phrase *xtin nuul ru uach na, xtin tzikij ru uach jumej chic,* which translates roughly as, "I will call her face forth once again, then you might see her face one time more." When someone returns from a faint or a serious illness, the Tzutujil say *xuul ruach,* "his face returns." The word for face and for the fruit, nut, seed, grain or the produce any plant puts forth is the same word. So essentially in making tentative promises to the Moon, the Hummingbird is saying," I will call forth her fruit again, you may see what she produces this time around."

This is all in reference, of course, to how a seed looks as opposed to the plant that it belongs to. Knowing how the possibility of a magnificent shady oak tree sleeps in the tiny heart of an acorn, the desperate Moon assumes that what the shaman will grow from her daughter's gathered pieces and "Heart of Fresh Water," will be the original form of the obedient child she lost.

In the same house where the Tall Girl was imprisoned, where the Water Daughter was dammed in, the Moon herself is now interned, confined like a mother bird to her nest at the direction of her son-in-law in order to hatch her daughter back to life.

In as much as they call their homes nests, the villages call their children nestlings and themselves nesters. The Moon's house is the world and her bed is the sky, and as a parent bird she is forced to "cook" her daughter into life. The idea is that the sacrificial cooking pot cooks both animal flesh and plant flesh which when consumed by the people actually does bring the people back to life by nurturing them. It is also understood that the *Rukux* that makes a seed grow when not killed by cooking or an animal to reproduce when not killed, is the same powerful force residing in the flesh of either that has the ability to give nutrition to those that eat of the plants and animals. When water is "cooked," it evaporates, or is killed, becoming clouds or steam which still contains this "heart" spirit force that rains back to the earth and feeds the plants which feeds the animals, all of which feed us humans. Thus the flesh of the Daughter of the Moon is water, which causes life to procreate and, when cooked, evaporates dismembered into the sky as life-giving rain, and in plants and animals, she feeds the world.

When the Moon begins to hatch her daughter, it is the force of Moon's pulsing time cycles that turns the hidden plant water and the girl's diverse spirit forms into various, immeasurable forms of animals.

Because, unlike plants, they can now move and make sounds on their own, the Moon mistakes all the forms her Daughter takes as a single form and keeps trying to open the pot. Moonlight tries to penetrate everything.

That there are thirteen nights to hatch the daughter actually refers to the twelve moons or months of the year and the residual thirteenth Moon that never quite fits into the solar year, coinciding only every fifty-two years. The Moon is hatching out the animal natures of the Earth's annual cycle, and as in all things Mayan, the plants are what give the animals unique natures.

Hatched into movement by the Moon, the world has a different nature every month as seen by the different plants and animals that grow, flower, die back, molt, give birth, migrate in each cycle of the Moon. Insects and birds in particular become the markers of the micro-times of the annual natural cycle, and each beast is considered to "own" little pieces of the cycle. Ever since then, the Ocean and the Sky have been in-laws, lightning goes with rain, and the land between the sky and the Ocean belongs to these many particular forms of the water Goddess.

Each of these animals are said to "call" into life that piece of the year, their respective chunk of time, if you will.

A certain bird, for instance, calls the wind of January, and another the fuchsia flowers and fruits out of the pitaya cactus of July, and another the pollen haze of certain days in March, and so on. It is the songs and movements of the animals that are said to make the annual cycle of all the myriads of natural changes of the world come into view.

When the Hummingbird cracks open the sacrificial pot with a stone, he is reenacting the lightning strike that kills his beloved, only this time with the patient diligence of a mature love instead of the violence of jealous hatred. Mayans have always smashed clay pots as a sacrifice at calendar shrines to feed specific calendar dates as living deities at the ends of initiations, signifying of course, like a bird, the emergence of the "new person" out of the pressure cooker of the cultural egg at a specific time of year.

In some versions of this tale, when the girl makes her cry out of the pot, she appears as an iridescent, oscillated turkey. In other, more modern recountings she comes as a peacock, which though not native to Guatemala, became a favorite among the Maya, ever since the Spanish brought them to their estates from Asia centuries ago.

The original story says that the girl emerged from the broken clay egg as a sleek "never-before-seen-bird" whom the Ocean sparkle,

Hummingbird Man, can now finally marry with complete freedom. Having outwitted the Moon and the Sun, the Gods of the jealous sky, he returns to hummingbird form to live with his beautiful bird-wife. Like all birds, to the Tzutujil, Hummingbirds and Horned Guans have the magical capacity to use their iridescence and songs to court into tangible life the characteristics of a certain time of year, like the sprout out of a seed, which in their case means the summer rains.

The word for a bird's song is *Tzikij*. This same word is used in prayers to mean "summoning into life," and more commonly it also means "to call forth" or "to court."

The story says that water and the souls of all things divine must be courted, listened to and truly seen. If we boss, control, contain, dam, overlook, assume or attempt to seduce the Heart of the World, then She will flee into a dismembered state and will then be seen by us only in the small and myriad particular forms of life's diversity.

What the story doesn't say, but every villager knows, is that every year the Moon makes love to the Sun in the middle of the sky, divides her heart in two and gestates another Tall Water Girl, and the story begins all over again.

Each year after a long dry season, Hummingbird goes courting Water with his exuberant sugar-brained trills, zooming around in a whirling suicidal flight. One Moon later when the thick, annual fog of Earth's sorrow hangs unmoving on the hills and the calls of his elusive sweetheart the Horned Guan haunt the spring mists of the deepest ravines, then the people know the story has been told, and the Rain of Grief and the Rain of Mother Waters is returning to call everything back to life.

Third Layer

Ecstasy and Time

Tzutujil Mayan shamans understand that every individual human being carries the entire Earth within their skins. Because they are what they are, they cannot understand why the rest of the world can't see that all the very same life forms, animals, plants, seen and unseen creatures, mountains, canyons, wet and dry plains, lakes, springs, rivers, caves, clouds, storms, winds, nights and days, lightnings, sun and moon, stars and a billion known and forgotten little things, who are sung alive and into form from five layers of previous Times on the big wide Earth, simultaneously chirp, roll, grow, die, argue, dream and hide in the same churning collective as our human body.

Maybe this inability to see such a thing has something to do with the verb "to be" and the Indigenous Soul of humans.

Growing up on the reservation in northern New Mexico, speaking a Native tongue most of the time and English only to my parents, I learned to speak to the world and about the world in a sophisticated, ancient language that did not contain the verb *to be*. Later, again, in Guatemala, speaking in Tzutujil and other Mayan dialects, I learned to listen and speak to a different world about the same world without a verb *to be*. I discovered over time that one of the things that distinguishes Indigenous cultures and provides a vision that is so friendly to their surroundings was that, strictly speaking, their language negotiated communication without the verb *to be*.

Because I am a native "non-to be" language thinker, I have never quite fully accomplished "to be" thinking and have spent my lifetime trying to get the stubborn horse of "to be" languages to carry the beauty of native "non-to be" understandings.

It would seem obvious at first for a language to function without a verb like *is, was, has been, are,* etc., it would have to be utterly relegated to the massive use of metaphor. While all native languages, like Maya Tzutujil, are filled with a constant and magnificent use of complex metaphors, it is even more necessary in a language such as English because of its massive dependence on the verb *to be*. Metaphors are the *only* way English could function without using the verb *to be*. The brilliant ingenuity of Indigenous language and what is indigenous in all languages, especially the language of origination, ritual and the sacred, though often mounted on rails of metaphor, is the way they zoom way past metaphor into realms of understandings that have metaphor looking rather naïve.

For languages like English, Persian, Norwegian, French, Italian, Greek, Russian, Hindi, Celtic or any other of the many, many Indo-European tongues with a strong causality-oriented verb *to be, metaphor* is the term these cultures use when speaking about the functions for which native cultures, like the Maya, have rituals. These "to be" cultures see native ritual as metaphors for the Universe, or the functions of weather, or fertility, etc. This, however, is not entirely accurate, though fairly sympathetic, considering that most "to be" cultures have dismissed their own indigenousity as some form of antique foolishness.

For Mayans, without a verb "to be," a ritual need not "be" a symbol or metaphor for something that it cannot "be" literally in a "to be" language like English. A ritual can "be" the universe, because the ritual and the universe can be the same thing. In this way our bodies are not metaphors of the Earth, they are the Earth. Ritual is what makes our bodies the Earth, and stories, like *The Daughter of the Sun,* are what show us the functions of the body of the ritual in order that we can ritually maintain the Flowering of the Earth and our bodies.

Because Mayans and most Indigenous people the world over are not burdened with the dilemma of "to be or not to be," as a matter of fact without a verb *to be* that's not even a question, they teach, learn, remember, keep alive, argue and respond to questions through stories.

Though one huge metaphor filled with an infinite flood of delicious, unfolding layers of metaphors within metaphors, deep ancient stories, like *The Daughter of the Sun,* are not really considered to be only metaphors in Mayan understanding.

They are really quite straightforward moving histories of our human souls in our bodies while simultaneously they are histories of ourselves in the Earth, and the story of the Earth inside the Body of the Holy, all at once, none mutually exclusive of the other.

Therefore stories like this one are not only metaphors for life, but more deeply they are the actual delicious liquor distilled from the cultural fermentation brought about by millennia of living ritually, spiritually on fire and at home fulfilling the primordial nature of the Indigenous Soul.

My understanding of the Indigenous Soul of humans began in my early days, tumbling over my hot, one-sided assumptions like a cold waterfall of melting ancient ice over the Sun's broiling head.

The people I was raised with on the reservation were not my blood relatives, and yet my own background had a home alongside thousands of indigenous Pueblo people. I learned early on that conformation to a race or a particular ancestry did not make a person indigenous. Though there are tribes, bands and villages of Native people all over the world who are closer to their Indigenous Souls than the mounting masses of people who have no idea of what that means, it is not the racial ancestry of these Indigenous people that make them indigenous. This insistence on making Indigenousity and Race the same thing is a stigma of people who have recently lost or anciently forgotten their relationship with the ground they stand on. Like the original Indian reservations, this stigma is designed to keep the indigenousity of modern people hidden like a refugee deep inside the landscape of their own Earth Bodies, far from the epicenters of their everyday consciousness, thereby avoiding the discomfort of the nagging feeling of grief about that loss.

The term *indigenous* is not an indigenous English word, but has a rather nice Latin ancestry whose parts *Inde* and *genous* anciently signify "inside" and "born," respectively. Over time it has come to mean similarly "native to a place."

So, indigenousity must refer to a person, plant, animal or thing who "belongs" to a place, something that is at home.

What is almost always erroneously translated from Tzutujil Maya into English as the verb *is* corresponds more correctly to the word *Ruqan* meaning "carries" or *Ruxin,* "belongs to."

Where as in English we might say, "That is how those people are," in Mayan we could only translate that sentence as *Ruxin wa ja vinaq,* which actually means, "It belongs to those people." When an American settler says, "This is my land, this land is mine," a Mayan would end up having to put it *Javra uleu rugan cavinnaq joj, ruxin joj ja uleu,* which comes out as "This soil carries my people, we belong to this land."

It's easy to see how easily the verb *to be* can be twisted to endorse a conqueror's mentality, and we would have to work consciously to make our language friendly to "belonging" to a place. People who do not know that the soil carries them in the same way a branch carries its fruit or that owning the land is much different than belonging to the land (not to mention utterly destructive to the land it pretends to own), make it very hard for their indigenousity to have a place to make any kind of a home on this earth, much less a land where they could actually feel "born into" or indigenous.

The Indigenous Soul then is that natural, nonhuman, spiritual origination place inside all beings, peoples, animals and plants that is older than anything ancestral, past the ancestral greatnesses and successes, past the ancestral ruts, prejudices and stupidity. The Indigenous Soul is the original place upon which our indigenous ancestors were carried, to which they belonged, filling them with any greatness they might have had. Their Indigenous Soul was what made them belong to the rest of the world of which they were a magnificent but small part.

Old Indians, Native people from all over the world and most of all our people's ancient ancestors will tell you that our Indigenousity is in the ground, in the water, in the Earth itself. And inside of us wherever that earth is found, it is there that our Indigenous Soul resides, waiting like a noble in exile.

It is from this indigenous place, this earth inside and outside our bodies, that our memory of how to be well in a place patiently waits. The Indigenous Soul of humans is the soul of being able to be truly at home as a human being.

Contrary to the hopes of old-time colonialists, socialists, fascists, neocolonialists of globalized capitalism or any number of fundamentalists, the Indigenous Soul cannot be killed by the usual means. Indigenous people, languages, plants, animals and places can be killed and destroyed, and continue to be annihilated and assimilated at a rate beyond present-day capacity to measure this travesty. However, because a peoples' Indigenousity is the flowering of the Indigenous Soul in those peoples, and the Indigenous Soul is not human and lives in the place behind the ground, beyond the water, the Indigenous Soul can be neither vanquished nor exterminated when Indigenous people, their Indigenous culture, Indigenous plants, animals, water or land are destroyed, settled or domesticated by disindigenized people who have had their own indigenous flowering forbidden and spiritually herbicided in the past by others like them before and others before them and so on.

This well established habit of driving the Indigenous Soul underground, as terrible as it is and has always been, also means that like a faithful lover, the Indigenous Soul is always waiting in great longing to return to us, where together we could be at home on this Earth, belonging to the place.

Because of its yearning for our company, the Indigenous Soul makes regular love forays into every individual's life, hoping to court our soul back to life. When it does this, it comes into our earth body in a personal form, which I call the Invisible Soul. The Tzutujil call this being your *Aj elbal,* or "that which comes out with you," referring to the day on which you are born when this invisible soul is born right behind you like a twin, though nobody can see it. Because it comes from the Indigenous Soul, it is not really a human thing but takes the form of something natural. Some people might even call the Invisible Soul our nature.

This Invisible Soul is every person's private envoy, sent by their pre-ancestral, origination point personified, i.e., their Indigenous

Soul, who in a pre-birth kind of arranged marriage lives together with our personal soul. Our personal soul lives inside the house of our forming body, while the Invisible Soul is everywhere in the oceanic brine that surrounds us, side by side in the womb.

In the story the Hummingbird is the Invisible Soul, and like our own Invisible Soul, what he is in love with is our watery, fresh-water soul that resides inside our Earth body.

This watery soul is what can someday become a more solid thing with its own unique form, but in the beginning, from the womb to the teenager days, like all watery things, this soul obeys the shape of whoever contains it.

For the Tzutujil Maya, to whom this story belongs, the world, the earth, the sky and everything in between is a magnificent house. If our bodies are the Earth, then our bodies are a magnificent house as well. What is this house built from and to whose plan is it constructed?

Like a village house, our bodies and the Earth use Time as its main building material, and it is constructed to the blueprint of ancestral memory. The solid parts of our bodies and the solid parts of the Earth are temple mansions made of regular, everyday Time as represented by the Sun in the story.

But the shape and the movement that go on within this house of solidified Time are under the tight and rhythmic direction of Ancestral Time. In the story we see her as the Moon, as cyclic Time, where she insists on doing things in a way that has already been done, then having run that cycle, must be done over the same way again.

This house of Regular Time and Ancestral Time is the House of the Sun and Moon, the Earth body within which lives our watery soul, Tall Girl in the story.

Because they are water, Tall Girl and our watery souls obey and conform to the shape, way of life and demands of Time in the House of the Sun and the Moon. But there is more to life than the House of the Sun and Moon, more kinds of Time than regular time and ancestral cycles.

Everyday time, constant time, waking time, work time, measurable time is all solar time as personified by the Sun. He is tall because this kind of Time is long and stretches out. Because it is long and tall and always going in one monotheistic, monocultural direction, this kind of Time has no "time" in which to see something as small, multidirectional and from another time, like the Hummingbird Boy, our Invisible Soul. It is not only the smallness and subtle nature of the Invisible Soul or Hummingbird that causes him to be unaccounted for at first and later banished from our bodies by the Sun and Moon.

Tzutujil say all life originated in the old time ocean. In our story the Indigenous Soul, like a deepwater beast, the Whale, hides in the Grandmother Ocean.

The Ocean in our story stands for the gathering of All Time, all types of Time in one huge churning swell. Because the Hummingbird Boy is the child of the Grandmother Ocean and the Whale, as the Invisible Soul he comes from the Indigenous Soul who lives in All Time Gathered.

Unlike her future in-law the Sun, whose Time only lives now, the Ocean is nonsequential time, time already done, time to come, time that will never happen, time that could have happened and more, all mixed into one large matrix of Gathered Time.

It is inside this immeasurable, pregalactic immensity where the Whale of the Indigenous Soul hides, and when the Sun's Regular-constant-one-direction-Time reflects on the ocean-wet surface of that Whale's long, rolling body, the Invisible Soul is born of that flash and released from Gathered Time, becoming a particular place in Regular Time, and comes ashore to our body and this world where, as a sparkling hummingbird, he courts and loves the fresh water of our body's Soul, who is still living inside a house made of

Constant Time and the cyclic urgency of ancestral form inherent in all Matter. These are two kinds of mothers, the Ocean and the Moon: the Ocean a matrix of all time, the Moon the cyclic nature of matter. The son of one courts the daughter of the other. Not only is matrix Latin for womb, but the English noun "matter" comes from the Latin word "mater" meaning "mother."

If the Ocean holds us in the womb, then the child of that Ocean, our Invisible Soul, surrounds us and talks beautifully to us there and we talk back. Like Tall Girl and Short Boy sitting on the threshold of the Body House of Time, we banter and enjoy beguiling each other with the pure joy of our togetherness.

Old Mayan midwives, matrons and moms refer to the cervix as the "threshold to the family compound"—in our story, the compound doorway to the Ancestral Hut of the Moon.

It is no wonder, then, that after floating forever in the Matrix-of-All-Time-Gathered, when birth comes and that water breaks and we are born into this dry, airy land that our Invisible Soul takes invisibly to the wind, becoming an airborne being, like the Hummingbird.

These same, venerable women in the village call the delivery of the old generous husk of the placenta and its umbilical cable and afterbirth, the Other Child, referring of course to the Invisible Soul born with the baby. They take great care with the delivered afterbirth, knowing it to be the spiritual remains of the previous life of one half of our being which has now been bodily separated from its pre-birth sweetheart.

On our wee heads at birth and for awhile after, a little boneless, skin-covered, semitriangular spot pulses, which is called in Tzutujil, *Ru yá*, meaning "his or her water." Mysteriously in English this place on a baby's head is called the fontanel, from the French meaning "little spring of water." Until this soft place seals and closes up, we as infants are able to continue with an everyday, troubadour-style love affair with our airborne Invisible Soul, who hovers nearby. But when this doorway of our body, like the house of literal Time of the Sun, hardens over with bone, the doorway is dammed up, our Watery Soul sealed inside. Like Tall Girl, our Watery Soul begins a long siege of yearning for its Invisible Soul locked out from our Time, our body and house.

Sometimes moments of great sadness and overwhelming melancholy overtake us and off and on we weep for that which nobody seems to see or can remedy.

In time our Watery Soul bears up under it and learns how to live inside, growing taller and gathering to it a great growing flood of soul whose diligence and creativity inside this House of Literal Time and Ancestral Insistence adds measureless amounts of childhood beauty and later, teenage mystery and extravagance to the body, which the Sun and Moon inside us somehow assume is their own.

Like Tall Girl, the abilities of our Watery Souls do not come from the Literal Time of the Sun, yet like plants heated by the glare of this same Time, our talents can mature. The fierce antique insistence of Ancestral Rhythm, which says we must do the same things that were done before us in Old Time, in the same way, in order to serve the Present Time of the Sun, is not the source of the creative magnificence of the Water Soul, but it does give it a dependable form against which to find its own expertise.

The Sun and Moon in this deeper understanding of the story are not our parents, but are things inside of us as part of our Earth body. Because water conforms to whatever form it is held in, and without the Invisible Soul to cause our imaginative Watery Soul to find its own ecstatic voice and personal form inside our body, the thinking that goes on in our body's head is the unimaginative literalist thinking of Present Time, the Sun who believes the situation as it appears on the eve of our spiritual revolution (of which he is totally unaware) is everything it should be and all it could ever be.

The Moon, on the other hand, is a pump, and like the Sun, a form of Time as well, but Time repeated instead of constant. She is the heart of our body. The heart is not the same as our Watery Soul, though it chases it around our body with a rhythmic insistence on regularity and conformation to the constant Time of the Sun. Because as the heart she is Repeating Time, she is Ancestral Time, and that kind of cyclic pump can only exist if it has a Watery Soul to work on.

This Time of Ancestral Insistence that the Moon represents applies not only to people but to minerals, plants, weather, animals, seasons and pretty much everything that the literalist Sun considers real.

Minerals consistently crystallize into ancestrally established patterns even after being ground up in rivers and wind, melted in volcanoes, spewed out and chewed by the ice, cooled again and pressed under a million, trillion tons of fellow rocks.

Pine trees consistently grow from strange, wispy, unarmored seeds, to ooze the same tar, crusty bark and leaves whose smells, cones and height are all caused by their stubborn ancestral insistence. It is this rhythmic appearance in certain specific ways, followed by a disappearance in another prescribed way, only to reappear in the first same way all over again, for which the Moon is so famous.

If the Sun as Constant Time is a literalist and semifascist, only looks forward and falls asleep when the soul has a problem, then the Moon as Rhythmic Time is the feeling of the heart, whose highly opinionated thinking is not only suspicious and proud but also fierce and guilty and above all anxious that things continue going in circles around a hub that stays put, which of course is her. She is not against change as long as it has already been an established change in the past.

The story says both this Sun and this Moon live inside us and are necessary parts of our Earth-Body-House. However, until our

Invisible Soul reappears, at first in our adolescence (maybe we get other chances later on if we miss that one), our Watery Souls, like Tall Girl, may become convinced in the interim that Regular Time and the Body and Ancestral Habit know everything there is to know and that what they want is what is right.

Not knowing any other kind of thinking, utterly strapped inside the natures of their individual restrictive Times, where things are not evaporated or eroded by living, both of these parts of us, the Sun and Moon, make watertight excuses as to why our Watery Souls will never marry away from them, why our souls can never move beyond their Time.

But ...

Though the beauty and imagination of the Watery Soul can be forced to serve any space and time, its generous and abundant nature cannot help but overflow the structures of Regular Time and the rigid, scheduled assumption of Ancestral Cycles.

When the stalk of a tall, hidden plant begins to flower, its perfume, like the deep song of a chained prisoner, rises over the prison walls, past the fortress of Present Time, over the heads of Ancestral Wardens, extending a subtle fish line of ecstatic longing onto which our Invisible Soul is hooked and reeled out of the memory of its former shape, transformed by the overflowing banks of our matured longing, into a shiny never-before-seen thing.

As a unique and subtle chunk of All Time Gathered, the Invisible Soul, like the Hummingbird, has had to wait until its womb sweetheart, the Watery Soul, found a way to puncture the dam of Regular Time to get past the Ancestral Cycles, thereby causing the body to change so that after his long wait this indigenous envoy from other times could find a subtle way in to our soul's Water.

Because all of this is our body, our minds, our heart, our soul, it is often our creativity, after years of spiritual dormancy or conformity, that carves this hole in the house of Regular Time to let a representative of a Time beyond Time into our body where, like Tall Girl and Hummingbird Boy, we are for a short while tearfully reunited with our invisible unseen part.

This is an incredible moment, a sort of spiritual honeymoon, but it is far too short. This is not to be confused with the arrival of a magical human being, or some kind of love affair with a person, though sometimes it begins by thinking it is.

The clandestine characteristic of this reunion between our Watery Soul and its equal unseen half comes from the terror of that part of us which has up until now imparted its form onto us. For it seems Regular Time and the Ancestral Mission to keep things as they are have no form of their own outside of their Time. They fear that our soul's wild love for a kind of Time unknowable to them will be an excursion into a formless death and a final melting away of our Time-made body and soul.

This fear comes from the fact that our Watery Soul has an ecstatic nature.

The word *ecstasy* comes down to us in English from the old Greeks, some of whom probably defined it much as we do today. From the root words *ek,* meaning "out, outside of" and *histanai,* "to place," ecstasy is still understood to be a state of being "out of the usual place, overpowered, transported or beside oneself with feeling and emotion, especially that of joy; a trance of delight or madness that arrests the whole mind."

The Old Greeks and their neighbors, though, knew that ecstasy was much more than that. Two other English words, *static* and *stasis,* come directly from the Greek word *histanai* as well. In stasis, *histanai* is still the infinitive of the verb "to stand" but now as water stands. *Stasis* as it is defined means, "to stop the flow of any liquid, water or blood, especially fluids in the body." *Static,* also from the word *histanai,* means "causing to stand, not moving or progressing, inactive, stationary."

This state of being transported by the feeling of joy, this ecstasy, then must come from being "outside of the detained flow of liquid in the body," or from being "outside of stasis," a flowing away from, standing still, outside of static Time especially the Time-built body.

Never having been outside of the hard structure of Regular Time and the unquestioned mandates of Ancestral Rhythms, the Watery Soul in an effort to follow its desire rushes madly behind the Invisible Soul, assuming the shape of the Myriad Things of the world. In a fast, convoluted run straight toward the eternally welcoming arms of the Infinite Matrix of Gathered Time, with no experience in freedom, having fled its literalist container of Simple Time, our Watery Soul confuses the initial euphoria of formless desire as ecstasy, and in the naiveté of this free-fall plunge, both parts of our souls head for the Matrix of Gathered Time in an instinctual effort to climb back into the womb to regain the timeless bliss of their original togetherness.

Once we are out of the womb the first time, our souls cannot return, but must take another route toward ecstasy, away from the womb, a route that leads to becoming a womb, a route towards a small and everyday form to make a throne for our Ecstatic Soul.

If our souls succeed in reaching the Ocean of All Time, both our Invisible Soul and Ecstatic Soul would cease to be different things and no longer yearn for each other. Merged into oneness, with all their differences mushed and homogenized, they would not have any of the small peculiarities and solid uniquenesses from which, as separate beings, they could give the other gifts. Neither would they have the friendship of two beings negotiating the mortal difficulties of living. Making love would be impossible, because coming together, receiving and giving, crying out in ecstasy, can only happen if they are distinct beings. This ecstasy of the Watery Soul and the Invisible Soul is not bliss, nirvana, happiness or euphoria; it is something very different.

If we are fortunate, and Chance and Chaos are doing their jobs, then a lightning flash from unexpected Sudden Time will rescue us from our soul's inability to resist its magnetic drift toward continued formlessness in the Matrix of All Time.

Running anywhere he wants, crisscrossing the path of the Sun, his brother's monodirectional Regular Time, the grumpy North Wind lives in Any Old Time causing unexpected and sudden things to happen.

The Tzutujil called it *Rax Caypat* , meaning "sudden or thorough lightning." This Sudden Time from Any Old Time is the dismembering, sacrificial knife of everyday life whose right and left hands are Possibility and Chaos.

Were it not for this lightning bolt of Sudden Time from Any Old Time, our Watery Soul could never become the Ecstatic Soul who is the only one who can be with the Invisible Soul.

It is Sudden Time which causes the deep desire of our potentially ecstatic Watery Soul to collide head-on with the profound grief of the Invisible Soul, thereby knocking us completely out of any kind of Time whatsoever. This is what ecstasy means, a soul that by passing through and wrestling every kind of Time gains a form that can exist outside of Time.

The deep desire of our Water Souls can turn into real love only if our initial form made of Regular Time and Cyclic Time is dismembered and reconfigured by Sudden Time on our way back to Womb Time such that the grief of our Invisible Soul from the Indigenous Origination Point in All Time can coax the Ancestral Heart away from its fundamentalist need to be right.

Working together in Regular Time, the magic of the Invisible Soul and the curiosity of the Ancestral Heart despite themselves create a Time that causes the layers of the Watery Soul to gestate in its own Time, from shape to shape, into its own particular never-before-seen ecstatic form. In its new, natural worldly form our soul can now love and sing to what it could formerly only desire: The Hummingbird of the Invisible Soul. It is this type of intelligent grief-tempered love that the new Ecstatic Soul has that makes the Indigenous Soul trust us and feel welcome. Its invisible messenger can now have a visible form, and together, not as one, but as lovers, they can be at home in service to the world in which our Earth Body lives.

This story is a chronicle of the distance and layers of Time that our Watery Souls must travel to achieve a particular living form that is solid, moving and useful to something unknown and bigger than human imagination. This story is about initiation, which says that after passing through five layers of Time, we find that our souls are ecstatic, magical, and particular and live in the space between All Time and Regular Time, in a place called No Time, and only then are we capable of love.

The story says that love does not make our lives easier, nicer or happier; it is an obligation, and ecstasy is a natural state in the movement toward that obligation.

Though the story doesn't say it in so many words, it is a given understanding in the deepest parts of Tzutujil tradition that every layer of Time in our bodies, the Earth and the Creation is actually a composite sound caused by the Deities of that particular strata of Time singing the songs of all the particular things, thereby causing them to materialize in this world as their diverse natures.

Everything is made out of sound. I and the bird that just flew by are just little knots of layered time made tangible by the ecstatic singing of wild and natural Gods.

It is also understood that each of these layers of Time must sing all together for the entire, crazy project of the Creation to fire up and function.

This creates a symphony of matter and movement and living things mixing in such an ornate and mind-boggling, alchemical magnificence as to be greater than the sum of its parts. In Mayan, this is called *Rax yá rukux kotzejal juyú ruchiuleu*, the Flowering Mountain Jade Water Heart.

As they are shown in the story, the layers run more or less as follows:

The Sun is the plodding of Regular Time carried from day to day whose unchanging monotonous sound is like the drone note of a bagpipe, or the khomei of a Mongolian throat singer, or the sound of a beehive, or the tamboura under a räg played on a sitar.

The Moon is the rhythmic, ancestral heart against whose complex and insistent cadence the Myriad Things of the world do moan, move and dance. She is the djembe, the tympani, the tabla, the creaking of crickets, the evenly spaced feathers on a bird's wing, the drumming of a rabbit's hind leg, the rings on a wild goat's horn, the crisscross ripples in a stream.

The Grandmother Ocean as All Time Gathered is the low humming sound of all things leaving and coming home, or the great swelling chorus of Georgian table songs that spread like deep layers of dolomite at the speed of forming marble.

The Lightning of Sudden, Unexpected Time from the North Wind who lives in Any Old Time is the frightening punctuation of cymbals crashing, the horrid yelps, snarls, barks and screams of an unforeseen dog fight, the abrupt sounds of scared water birds rising away from the eagle, the sounds of cliffs pulling apart and trundling into canyons, volcanic eruptions, the rage of a mother bear with her head stuck in a bucket, the tongue of a toad, a skunk on a piano, a visit from an apologetic enemy.

The Hummingbird, the Invisible Soul, is the Time of Possibility whose sound is the sound of dragonflies who, finally hitting the air after years as nymphs in the water, play violins made from the tail-hairs of the wild horses of grief; who together with the Ecstatic Soul is Time out of Time, whose song is The Story of The Daughter of the Sun whose lyrical melody holds this symphony of Time together.

Her song is the flowering on the stalk, the water drop on a duck's blue wing as he waddles out of the marsh, slow steam rising from a puddle in the desert where overnight micro-frogs with red eyes appear, the insane ideas of ground squirrels who think they can disappear by simply having the exact same color as the fence post on which they perch motionless; She is the sound of a wild sword fight between two boys in love with the same girl who end tired and unwounded, weeping in each other's arms; She is the sound of the mad dreams of some of this world's people who still think that the mountains are fed by her story and cause the hilly grass to grow and the waters of the spring to crash back to the sea.

Fourth Layer

Never-Before-Seen Bird

Up on the Pacific Northwest coast of North America, amongst the thickly treed tops of a rocky jumble of islands poking past the mists and loons, there was a man I'd known who could never smile.

He'd killed too much back in a Southeast Asian war. Only a twenty-year-old boy then, like a hand-fed trained falcon, he was sent dropping from the sky alone, parachuted repeatedly behind the lines, assassinating and wreaking havoc, until finding his way back to some predetermined point, he was gathered back up into the sky, helicoptered to a ship and rested, only to be sent out again and again. After cutting so many throats and terrorizing the lives of so many people he didn't even know, his sanity demanded he throw himself into the cold sea to die.

By the time they'd fished that tired killing-bird from the ocean and brought his heartbeat back into his chest, all the death he'd made in those early days and the grudge he bore his rescuers was fossilized into his face as one permanent frown that pretended not to care.

His own eyes unable to shed a drop, this man lived for years as a walking frozen tear. With no eye big enough to weep out what the country should have helped him do, but didn't, he waited for the climate to change so he could melt back into the ocean to forget and finally be forgotten.

For this, all the womenfolk that loved him dragged the poor man in to see me, at my camp, where I lived with my own grudge, out in the bush, shortly after returning from Guatemala; they figured maybe I could unfreeze him and help him find his smile. But I knew how that much grief would kill him in volume alone if expressed in less than fifteen lifetimes. No one seemed to understand what a sacrifice and service he did the rest of his family by accumulating all their inherited, ancestral sorrows along with his own, frozen in him alone, so the rest could live out their lives in an assumed normality.

Whether he thought it up on his own or it was something that came out of things we did, I can't remember anymore, but all of a sudden after his third visit or so, this speechless man without a smile, with a glazed stare like a petrified frog and frozen viper frowns, began recording bird songs.

But not until he showed up again after a long disappearance with recordings filled with the fierce miniature chortlings and sparkling zings of certain South American hummingbirds did I see his face begin to thaw. He didn't smile exactly, but in place of ice, an expression of demonic zeal toward a secret purpose had settled in.

On some sophisticated taping machine he slowed down the hummingbird songs until they were almost a set of subsonic twinklings.

This man then found his way as a crew member onto a mammal research ship surveying the Pacific waters in and out of the coastal islands off western Canada.

After weeks of keeping low and doing his job, he managed to convince one of the investigators to broadcast his slowed-down South American hummingbird songs beneath the sea to see what might happen.

For days on end, pods upon pods of whales of every kind came rolling in, breaching and blowing along side the ship, diving and gathering around the underwater speakers, chattering, hooting and cooing in courteous, measured replies between the hummingbirds' phrases.

Slightly chagrined, the elated ship's research personnel recorded the whales' exuberant conversation and after speeding them up found themselves listening to some very ornate hummingbird songs!

This man began to smile a smile that threatened to break his unaccustomed lips and stretched so deep that he wept off and on for years. But that day when this tiny warrior-bird of the air was thrust into the waters of the Grandmother Ocean, he was drowned in the whales' friendship. Those great ecstatic lords of the Grandmother Ocean chose to live in a sea of liquid grief long, long ago, and their friendly old songs sang the smile back into the drowning bird.

If our souls are truly made of fresh water and like disobedient girls long to run into the arms of the ocean, so must the tears we shed, when our dreams are kept imprisoned, be relatives of the sea. Let every teardrop be a footprint of our invisible soul swimming toward just such a welcome in our unaccustomed arms.

Fifth Layer: The Ecstatic Voice

A Revolution of the Watery Soul

The Sun is getting hotter, our icy poles are melting, their shores are pulling back. The water of the oceans rises and yet the bigger rivers are all diverted, enslaved and dammed. Some are sucked dry to water overgrown, polluted cities and domesticated land and never reach the sea, their deltas looking back wondering, while other rivers drag toward the ocean exhausted, thick, embittered with poison, dreaming of the hills and rain they came from.

If the Earth's watery soul cannot run toward the sea, then neither will ours inside our own Earth bodies. We will be stranded with a single kind of thinking who thinks its time is the only time and doesn't care how many other times, past or future, it wrecks to keep this time alive. This is the thinking of the hot Sun.

When lightning cracks the air, it dismembers the water in it, making ozone, which like the dismembered Daughter of the Sun diffuses the Sun's single-minded glare into a life-promoting warmth.

As collective tenants sealed in the ancestral cemeteries of former seas, old shellfish become petroleum, which is the living ocean's memory of what it was, whose story is told today in the swimming of her fish, the underwater flying of turtles, the gurgling of whales, the neurosis of crabs, the waiting of coral, the sucking of mussels and the tentacled preparedness of eternally frightened squid.

When we burn the ocean's oily memory to fuel our crustacean-like cars that carry us to jobs from where the Ecstatic Soul is banned, to pay for lives in which we are still never really at home, then together with the ocean, our memories darken the sky as smoke. While our futures burn up together, the deep teaching stories of our people and the oceans of All Time Gathered go hide with the children in a so-called fairy story or in small things where the power hungry never look.

The smoke of these burning memories kills the air, the ocean and the water, taking ozone from the sky, leaving us without the ecstatic vision, and alone with unbuffered Hot-Sun-thinking whose grace-less objectivism dams the water of the Earth and the water of our cultural grief, keeping it from its natural run to the sea and ecstasy. That thinking consumes its memories and stories like it consumes the world to avoid hearing the sound of its daughter's weeping over the sound of its crunching jaws.

Therefore, I say, when we speak stories and understand their depth, when we speak deep language, keeping it alive, we keep our memories from being burned, the ocean from being drilled for oil, with the ecstatic ozone between us and the glare of this Time.

The Ecstatic Soul in people and the route it must be allowed to take toward the Indigenous Soul is what could keep the ocean from having to come ashore to search for us and our Watery Souls from freezing into ice.

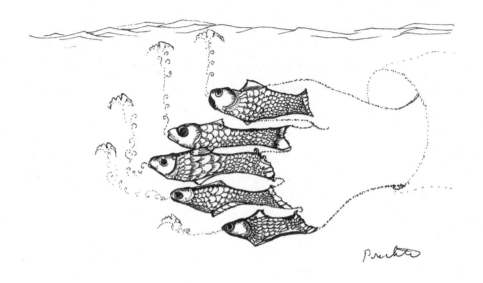

AUTHOR'S NOTE

A story such as this is a living organism and like all of us needs to eat.

To be fed it must be read aloud. So please, read it out loud to the young; read it to the old; read it to the middle-aged; read it to the sick; read it to the incredulous; read it to the polluted lakes; read it out loud to your dead ancestors; read it out loud over the phone to someone you can't be with; read it to an unhappy, human-ravaged, tired hunk of land; read it to your sweetheart; read it aloud to your keepers and wardens, whether they be your bosses, ancestral prejudices or a man with keys and a gun; read it to your father; read it to your mother. Above all read it aloud to yourself, especially that part of you that no one seems to see, and then the next time you have a chance to go to the water, give a new loaf of bread to the ducks, pigeons, a homeless woman or menacing raccoons, say, "Please story, receive a little of the original Flowering Earth, jump up and live again."

And know then that those refugees at the edge of our villages are teeth in the mouth of the Watery Soul of the Earth, whose Divine Indigenous Nature also lives forgotten at the edge of our hearts and is thereby fed a bit by the gesture, the Divine who so richly feeds us with her story.

All Blessings ...

Martín Prechtel

July 2001

Gavilan, New Mexico

GLOSSARY OF MAYAN WORDS

Though at one time certain Mayan dialects had written forms, some of which we know today from the remains of carved stone temples and stelae, a few rare writings on pounded paper now housed in European museums and on magnificent pottery, it is doubtful that this hieroglyphic writing was ever used for any casual everyday purpose. Most certainly writing of this sort was a ritual activity made for the benefit of the other world and not so much for humans.

Like Indigenous languages throughout the world, Tzutujil is a rich oral institution. In the recent past those who have decided to commit Tzutujil words to written symbols have composed as many orthographies as there were people wanting to write them.

While most of these writing systems use phonetic approximations derived from an already existing assignation of sounds from

German, Spanish, English, etc., which employed some form of the Roman alphabet, others have been completely new ornate inventions of the kind once popular with our most solemn linguists, but impractical for popular use.

Except in one instance that I know about, all attempts to put Tzutujil into writing were carried out by people who did not speak Tzutujil or any dialect of the many Mayan languages and created for the most part on behalf of non-Tzutujil academics, who wanted to have a way to complete their studies and so forth. In none of these instances was the writing system developed for the use of the Mayan people.

The one serious attempt where three Tzutujil speakers compiled dictionaries of their own languages was still at the instigation of an American linguist using his own orthography, but unfortunately it never resulted in a writing system for Tzutujil speakers.

Because the greatness of a language is in its speaking, its sounds cannot be truly written, they must be heard. The glossary that follows is only here as an attempt to show a little bit of the subtle depth and vast beauty of indigenous thought contained in the spoken Tzutujil. Though approximate, it uses symbols that have come to be commonly accepted for writing highland Mayan words.

The letter *x* is pronounced as "sh." Letters such as *Q* , *C* , *Tz*, *T* , *a* , etc., represent beautiful Tzutujil sounds not present in any European language. All other letters are pronounced as in Spanish.

Ajaua : Tzutujil Mayan for Lords, owners, or Gods, male or female. Plural of Ajau.

Ajelbal: Tzutujil Mayan for our natural soul that lives in nature, outside of us, and inside our Earth Body. Born invisibly with the afterbirth, it usually has the nature of an animal, plant or kind of weather. Literally, *Aj-elbal*, " He/she that comes out together."

Bney Tzij: Tzutujil Mayan for a storyteller, literally "word maker," but equally, "maker of truth."

C Tie Ya : Tzutujil Mayan for "Our Mother Water," a term of respect used for Lake Atitlan. The Goddess of the Lake.

Caypa Ch ú : Tzutujil Mayan for a whale, means literally "lightning fish." God of Hurricanes in the story.

C iac Tunuun: Tzutujil Mayan for a large, shy jungle bird once thought to be extinct, but who lives on in the isolated cloud forest regions of Guatemala. This striking bird is called in English by the strange name, horned guan, which refers to the beautiful fleshy, iridescent, ruby-colored hornlike headdress that sits on its head between its beak and the eyes. Tall Girl becomes a *C iac Tunuun* in her final transformation out of the clay pot. They always go in pairs, male and female, and are very loyal.

C wa Ya : Tzutujil Mayan for mountain springs of fresh water. They are Goddesses.

Huraqan: Tzutujil Mayan for hurricane or heavy rain. Literally "one foot." Europeans and Americans get their words for these tropical storms directly from the Mayan language.

Kiem: Tzutujil word for a backstrap loom. Backstrap looms have been in use in Mesoamerica for at least a couple thousand years. An assemblage of specific sizes, shapes and types of smooth wooden sticks, ingeniously held together by the warp and the cloth themselves. Traditionally used only by women. It is they who are responsible for the intricate magnificent cotton clothing made from weavings they do on the *kiem.* Though Mayans weave wool on the backstrap looms in Chiapas, traditionally cotton of many colors has been in use for a very long time. I have seen clothing made of milkweed silk, kapac and other wild, natural fibers.

Kilajtzij: Tzutujil Mayan for beautiful speech. Literally, "delicious word." Sometimes used sarcastically as if to say "that would be nice if it were true."

Pinol or *P nul:* Tzutujil from Toltec. A traditional Mayan beverage made from toasted corn and spices. Before the advent of the coffee culture, *pinol* was the most commonly prepared drink.

Pót: (to rhyme with coat) Tzutujil word for a Mayan woman's blouse, for which the Nahuat term *huipil* is commonly used internationally and in Spanish to denote the same. There are hundreds of types of *pót,* among all the different Mayan villages and language groups throughout the Mayan region, but the Tzutujil everyday *pót* reaches to the mid-calf and is covered to the waist by a wrap-around skirt called *uuq.* They are usually embroidered or woven with significant designs. A very ancient clothing form still found in use throughout Mesoamerica.

P tix: Tzutujil Maya for an ancient shape of fired clay cooking pot that is very large, egg-shaped, round-bottomed with a small opening at the top, and used to cook *suban* and sacrificial dinners. Like the world over, every type of pot has a specific name and function; there are a great number of designations among the Highland Maya.

Qan tí: Tzutujil Mayan word to denote the extraordinarily venomous bushmaster snake, *lachesis mutus.* Sometimes called *fer-de-lance* in English and *nahuayaca* in Spanish. Literally, yellow bite, in reference to this powerful beast's yellow chin. They are fearless and don't flee. Very few people survive their bite. Said by some storytellers to be one of the animals the Tall Girl turned into as she changed forms from one animal to the next in the pot.

Quetzalito: Spanish word from the Nahuat, *Quetzal.* Means little Quetzal bird. A type of hummingbird with long, tiny, iridescent tail feathers, reminiscent in tiny scale to those of the Quetzal bird, or magnificent trogon.

Rukux: Tzutujil Mayan for heart, placenta, center and germ of a seed, more specifically the spirit in anything that causes it to grow into a new form from a seed through all the changes back into many seeds.

Rumux Ruchiuleu: Tzutujil Mayan for belly button of the Earth, meaning the town of Santiago Atitlan and lake Atitlan as the center of Tzutujil universe. Literally, "the umbilicus of the face of soil."

Sotoy or *stoy:* Tzutujil word for an ornately woven cloth approximately two feet wide and four feet in length carried by women and girls as shawls in their daily errands, but distinguished from the much bigger shawls used only for courting and dressing up in that they are used as drying towels and often twisted and coiled to put under round-bottom water jars to prop them up and on the head to balance and cushion the jar while being transported. In Mayan ritual they are usually understood to be the Moon's serpents. Indeed there is a powerful large snake named *Sotoy* with beautiful markings on her back.

Subán: Tzutujil Mayan for a rectangular, ceremonial corn cake similar to a flat tamale made by steaming a hand-ground new corn which is wrapped in the long leaves of the corn stalk, not the shucks. They have lines down the middle and are very holy in all ritual feasts.

Touj ("j" pronounced as very breathy "h" sound): Tzutujil word for the traditional, rectangular steam bathhouse made by women from stones, mud and timbers inside of which a fire is set under a neat pile of volcanic stones. After the rocks inside are white hot, the ashes are scraped out, the people go in, a blanket is draped over the small entrance and cold water is dashed over the sizzling stones.

Short handfuls of switches with the leaves still attached are used by the bathers to direct the very fierce heat to specific parts of the body. Every traditional compound has a *touj*, though they vary in capacity from a two-person to a huge eight-person size. Sometimes called, in Spanish, by the Nahuat term *temezcal*. Owned by the women, it is a spiritual tool of the midwives and very relaxing for all genders.

Tq aq u ("q " pronounced as guttural clicking "g" sound): Tzutujil Mayan for a thick, square, hand-woven cloth from a meter to 150 centimeters on a side, whose corners are tied together to enclose a cargo. Refers also to a floridly adorned miniature form of the same used to transport tortillas and to keep them warm.

Tzimai: Tzutujil Mayan for one of three types of very resilient bone-colored gourds which originates as the fruit on certain thorny tropical begonia trees. After being hollowed out, the gourds are used as ceremonial vessels of various types. Their use is ancient and full of meaning. They are called *morro* in Guatemalan Spanish.

Tzutujil: Quiche Mayan word for an indigenous Guatemalan people who call themselves what all Mayans call themselves, *vinaaq* or "people." The Tzutujil are Mayans who number between fifty and sixty thousand people, all of whom live south of Lake Atitlan. The bulk of Tzutujil live in Santiago Atitlan and are for the most part a lakeside people. *The Disobedience of the Daughter of the Sun* is a version of one of their traditional stories.

Xcamiel ("x" is pronounced "sh"): Tzutujil Mayan for the southern lake wind, whose gentle breezes are warm and bring in the rainy season. Opposed to *Q iq* , the harsh, stormy, dry north wind.

Yaal: Tzutujil Mayan for a string bag usually made of maguey cactus fiber by Tzutujil men and widely used by them to transport what they grow and gather. One type, called *chbiyaal,* is actually made like a net. This is the netted bag used by the Hummingbird to bring home his sweetheart's remains.

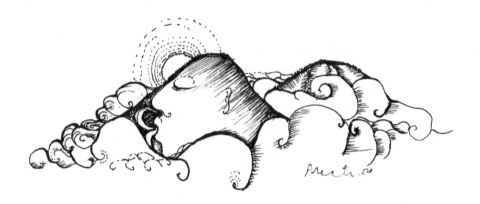

ACKNOWLEDGMENTS

People who say villages are what we need today have obviously never had to live in one! They probably come from big cities or the strange isolating failure of their suburbs where the insatiable hole of meaningless details of lawn chemicals, matching outfits, dead food and bad air from unpaid-for cars necessary just to keep afloat in the lonely synthetic soup of machine-dependent comfort, keeps them as individuals constantly struggling against invisibility, where daily one can painfully watch the beauty of their culturally neglected natural hearts bulldozed by the one-sided sham of television's trance-like promise of real communication into the morass of shallow thought, look-alike clothing, mass-produced accents, facial expressions and language, where life is acted out for effect instead of lived to feed the Divine. Perhaps because that kind of synthetic culture considers its mirror-sided punch bowl of neurotic complication as an irrefutable reality and, in an attitude of peculiar superiority, stereotypes the world's villages as small, simple-thinking places with unstressful lifestyles, certain people hearing the call of their natural hearts trying like grasshoppers to spring out of that toxic mixing bowl of modern comfort toward a life with real people in real places, imagine that in one of the world's villages life would be easier, their children and their own feelings given a more personal and significant existence. This would probably be true to some extent, but true culture cannot be obtained nor commodified for user-friendly consumption because, of course, that's just tourism or in some languages foreign invasion.

However, all that being said, when it comes to the considerations of the Bigger Picture, the only real differences between a small tribal village and the huge spread of commercial consumer culture are size, an addiction to comfort and modernity's glaring hatred of beauty.

For villages, like all places where humans would be the center of their own attention, are hard on the indigenous soul and harder still to the Earth.

Tzutujil Mayan traditionalists understood this perfectly, fully aware that every year they would have to intentionally collapse their village because, otherwise like big cultures and big cities everywhere else, the village would begin to consume its people and the surrounding land that fed it.

In order to tie together a village devoid of the old village's annual toxicities, every year at the same time, a community would form from among the people, who now considered themselves homeless refugees.

This community of ex-villagers came together to ritually and poetically feed the Heart of the Earth that fed them and take care of what the "village" always seemed to forget. The community that came out of this understanding would gradually congeal into a hierarchal village once again, a village that would have to be ritually and intentionally dismantled the following year and remade again through community.

Villages then are not by nature communities; villages come from humans wanting what they want. Communities come from losing villages.

Like the Never-Before-Seen Bird, community has to do with loss and a willingness to fail. It is fueled by grief, which forces our insistent desires to mature into a love for the small and forgotten. Community is a thing of Nature, not people, unless people are part of that Nature. Community is where individuals come flooding together to spiritually feed that big thing that feeds the village. It is about gratitude and ecstasy. Community is the ecstatic voice that lingers after the villages we insist upon are torn apart.

I have lost every village of which I was ever a part, and in those losses, great chunks of who I thought I was and the things I thought I knew were torn away, ground to dust and hurled afar.

This tiny, unchewable piece that the Jaws of Life left unswallowed was planted in that dust. One of the things that sprouted there is this book, but only because it was given a climate generous to its kind by a dispersed village of people who love the Watery Soul.

Though they are spread across this grand, Holy world, I would like to thank, toast and acknowledge the following people, for they form a house of collective friendship under whose roof this book did gestate into the never-before-seen form it has become.

First and always foremost, my most beautiful, curly-headed wife, Johanna, in whose generous heart I was sung and wept back to life. Without her love, patience and determined loyalty, her multiple abilities and her maintenance of enormous class under fire, I would not even be alive and none of this book would've ever been. I love her and I toast her as my only love and sweetheart, forever.

If that spread-out community is a house of friendship, then Ruth and Robert Bly are the intelligent and soulful doorway without which most of the people who follow here I would never have known. My best friends, always.

For Fred Berry the ecstatic geologist, whose love for the deep, ancient earth and the people who understand his love is almost as great as his love for his wife, Joanne, an inspiration to me and all who know him.

Orran Fisher, from South Dakota, who is probably one of my greatest fans, for whom I have great affection, once told me, "Why bother reading things that ain't true, like fiction, when you can read true things like yours that read like fiction?" All Blessings, friend.

Marianne Lust, Deborah Lubar, Mira Verner-Lust, eye-ball to eye-ball, keeping that place open in the walls of these times.

Tom Verner and Janet, my friends and my brother in the struggle for beauty and the Divine.

Sobrinos hermanos, Vicente Griego and Levi Romero, nunca dejadnos de luchar en servicio al duende, hacia la voz extática.

Miguel Rivera y Stefanita compadres de vivir con pasión.

Guy Jean, the poet, and his wife, Violette, big-hearted friends in the struggle to make oblivion roll over and let us tickle its belly.

To all the poets and their families: Thomas Smith, Judyth Hill, Jay Leeming, William Ayot, Coleman Barks.

Poet Fran Quinn, the enforcer of eloquence.

For Jim Watt and the Blake class at Butler University.

Eliza Rosales, mil gracias por su intelegencia y su amor por Machado (Northern Arizona University).

Reza Derakshani, whose ecstatic Persian singing of story, setar, kemence and nei, a music that melts weapons made of hatred into seeds of grief and possibility. Brother and friend always.

For David Whetstone, who understands the symphony of Time.

Anna Warrock, for copy editing and support.

Janene McNeil, for how she listens and all she gives.

For RP Jeff Harbour, a patient, living sattva if ever there was one, without whom we should most surely be lost. All Blessings.

For David Abram, Grietya and little Hannah. All Blessings.

For Felipe Ortega, for his love of desert water, sparkling earth and the ancient sacred nature of New Mexico.

For Craig Ungerman and Camille Benjamin, who know that the head is lumber from which to build a home for two hearts.

Marilyn Bacon, Chris, John and Annie, magical front-line lovers of the human heart. All Blessings.

Good friend Enhtur Ayush, for his morin khuur and mutual love of his homeland. Brothers always. Ikh bayarlalaa minee dhuu.

Diane Miller, Jim, David and family, Wick Fisher and Karen for their courageous help in the Big-Foolish-Project, their love of story and for their story.

For my beautiful son Santiago, singer of the ecstatic soul, a story for him, from his people.

For my beautiful son Jorge, lover of the Divine.

My father George, for his writing he did when I was a child, and his love of mine today.

For my brother John, a man of books, music and birds.

Tom Keller for his friendship, love of stories and the love he shows his daughter, my wife.

For all the initiates from Minnesota, Vermont, California, Guatemala, Canada and England who are made of stories. All Blessings.

For all my people, friends, supporters, neighbors from New Mexico, especially for Robert Alire and Lezlie King, cedar and indigo, borregos y chicos, for your friendship and help; Tim Viereck and family.

In Oregon all the friends and supporters, in particular:

In Portland, The Looking Glass Bookstore; Marlena Smith and

KBOO, Aryeh Hirschfield and family. All the friends in Bend, especially Sweet Medicine Nation and Mare Shey. In Eugene, the students and teachers of Eugene High School; Sally, Ted, Nathan and Christa Lowe; for their enormous intelligence, heart and listening, Vip Short and Tsunami Bookstore. In Ashland, Richard Seidman and Rachael Resch.

All the folks in Arizona: Jerry and Marjorie Dixon, Alegra Alquist, Shirley Tassencourt, and all the old generous Grandmothers.

People of Northern California, especially San Rafael, Sonoma, Point Arena, Elk, Casper, Mendocino and Arcata. All Blessings, you are never forgotten.

All the friends from the Minnesota Men's Conference.

For the friends and communities in Vermont, each of you like a feather on the bird of possibility flying courageously toward a nest of time, out of time, beyond ourselves, to hatch an egg of a never-before-seen thing. This book is for each of you. All Blessings.

For the Great Mother Conference: a sanctuary of imagination and story where a Jew, a Muslim and a Catholic can still pray together.

For all the plant people at the Green Nations and throughout the world, who know, like the Mayan know, that plants are water and water is first.

In particular, I would like to send a breath of life and blessing to the brave, diligent and soulful individuals and friends who attend the Ojo Caliente Writer's Retreat and the Vermont Writer's Retreat. It is there that this book really got started.

In the United Kingdom: All Blessings to Mark Goodwin and his family in Chelsea, London. Without his dedication, hospitality and foresight our continued returns to the England could never have happened.

My friend and a warrior-like ally who can be trusted with the spoken word as a way to feed the Holy, the ground, the people and the possibility of an intact indigenous life, Shivam O'Brien from Galway, Ireland.

For all the friends in Leeds, especially for Steve, Lyle and family.

For Carole Miles, Annie Spencer and John Scaife and all you wild beauties from the New Sap in the Old Tree Conferences. All Blessings.

In London, a toast to Marc Rylance, Claire VanKampen and family, and all the friends at the Globe Theater for all the courageous and gorgeous work you do on behalf of the spoken word, story and music, and especially for your friendship.

In Wales, with enormous affection and respect, Father Christmas, Leighton Davies and Ruth; Malcolm Davies and Claire; Nick Clemens, Mande, Tom and Anna; Allan and Gwyneth and family, the last man to make concert harps by hand in England, this kind of thing must never be forgotten. My book in honor of your harps, brother. Ave Da.

For the Tzutujil Maya people of the town of Santiago Atitlan, Guatemala, especially in memory and honor of all those old men and women, my teachers, relations, friends and colleagues, for the most part all passed on, who I neither forget nor dishonor, that whatever is written be only to strengthen the possibility that the stories stay relevant to life, not be lost or preserved only as cultural relics or nationalist prizes testifying to the demise of the Indigenous brilliance.

May the stories somehow live beyond the amnesia of the present times.

Utzlaj jie achinaq chiwe xix. Kamic majun chic n co tzra , taq nukux nbison chic ruman, taq ja rumaq kin tzibaj ja buj, ruman majun xtcamstaj rutzij rilaaj ojer vinaaq, ajni jaura xi bin chwa nen.

Matiosh chiwe, siwan tinamit.

And last I must thank Robert Smyth of Yellow Moon Press for initially publishing this beautiful book.... and my deep thanks to

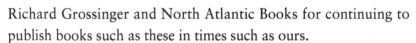

Richard Grossinger and North Atlantic Books for continuing to publish books such as these in times such as ours.

And anyone else whose name I should have mentioned, please receive this book as my thanks to you. All Blessings.

Kilab utzilab, utzlaj bey colo, majun loulo´, oxlajuh matioxiil.

ABOUT THE AUTHOR

A master of eloquence and innovative language, Martín Prechtel is a leading thinker, writer and teacher whose work, both written and oral, hopes to promote the subtlety, irony and pre-modern vitality hidden in any living language. As a half-blood Native American with a Pueblo Indian upbringing, his life took him from New Mexico to the village of Santiago Atitlan, Guatemala. There, becoming a full village member of the Tzutujil Mayan population, he eventually served as a principal in that body of village leaders responsible for instructing the young men in living out the meanings of the ancient stories through the rituals of adult rights of passage. Once again residing in his native New Mexico, Martín teaches at his international school, "Bolad's Kitchen." Through story, music, ritual and writing, Martín helps people in many lands to retain their

diversity while remembering their own sense of place in the daily sacred through the search for the Indigenous Soul. For further information, visit www.floweringmountain.com.

ABOUT THE ILLUSTRATIONS

Martín Prechtel is well known as an artist in Guatemala. His drawings and paintings have come to be an added gift and expected part of all his literary works.

All the illustrations in *The Disobedience of the Daughter of the Sun,* as well as the cover painting, are Martín Prechtel originals. The clothing styles and appearances in the book come from the Atitlan lake region in Guatemala as it looked fifty years ago and past. The little talking bird at the top of each page comes from a petroglyph pecked into the basaltic rocks of the region and was the pre-European marker for Tzutujil territory. It represents an ancient division of the Tzutujil people now obscured, called the Tzikin jai , or Village of Birds. For the most part these exquisite petroglyphs, like our stories and Indigenous memory, have been lost, as the basaltic boulders upon which they were written are split and crushed into building stones for American churches and tourist hotels. I include the little birds here, so despite their loss in the visible world, they can continue to mark the edges of the spiritual territory of Ancient Tzutujil Indigenous understandings as represented by the story in this book.

About North Atlantic Books

North Atlantic Books (NAB) is a 501(c)(3) nonprofit publisher committed to a bold exploration of the relationships between mind, body, spirit, culture, and nature. Founded in 1974, NAB aims to nurture a holistic view of the arts, sciences, humanities, and healing. To make a donation or to learn more about our books, authors, events, and newsletter, please visit www.northatlanticbooks.com.